Library of
Davidson College

EDUCATION
AND
ECONOMIC GROWTH

Education
and
Economic Growth

Fritz Machlup

UNIVERSITY OF NEBRASKA PRESS · LINCOLN

Copyright © 1970 by the University of Nebraska Press

All Rights Reserved

International Standard Book Number 0-8032-0746-8
Library of Congress Catalog Card Number: 74-105645

Manufactured in the United States of America

TO MY READERS

Preface

This essay is a greatly expanded version of a public lecture given on March 5, 1969, as one of the special events during the centennial-year celebrations at the University of Nebraska. Needless to say, less than one-third of the material presented here was included in the lecture.

When the invitation was extended to me, both the topic and the level of technicality were designated: I was to speak on "Education and Economic Growth" and my lecture was to be intelligible to an audience made up largely of noneconomists, yet at the same time interesting to a sizable contingent of professional economists. It was clear at once that this was too tall an order and that both groups in the audience would have to be merciful in judging the performance. Of course, in an oral delivery a friendly smile or a dramatic gesture from the speaker can tide a listener over unintelligible technicalities or familiar commonplaces. On the printed page, however, the technicalities may look formidable to the nonspecialist and the commonplaces strike the specialist as intolerable. Thus, I am afraid that I risk pleasing neither—unless both manage to skip the offending passages or sections.

FRITZ MACHLUP

Princeton, New Jersey

Contents

	page
Preface	vii
Introduction	1
I. The Productive Contribution of Education	5

Factors in Economic Growth; Assessing the Contributions to Growth; Education and Size of Labor Force; Education and Population Growth; Unproductive and Counterproductive Education; Fast Pay-Off: Training on the Job and Adult Education; Private and Social Returns; Differences in Private Incomes and National Product; Isolating the Effects of Education; The Findings; Working Hours and Leisure Time; Additional Social Benefits; Rates of Return Calculated for Soviet Russia

II. The Demand for Education   63

Indices of the Use of Educational Services; International Comparisons; Comparing the Quality of Education; Educational Growth in the United States; Disentangling Increases in Demand and in Cost

III. The Cost of Education   83

Total Expenditures, Cost of a Given Task, Cost per Unit; Scrambled Measures of Cost; Human Costs Rising with Economic Growth; Growth with Inflation; The Prospects

Index   101

EDUCATION
AND
ECONOMIC GROWTH

Introduction

The literature on the subject of education and economic growth is some two hundred years old, but only in the last ten years has the flow of publications taken on the aspects of a flood. A special bibliography published in 1966 listed almost eight hundred items, exclusive of studies concerned with particular countries; and at least ninety percent of the listed titles had appeared since 1960.

Many of the titles refer to "development" rather than "growth," and we should perhaps ask whether these two words have different meanings. To many authors the two words are synonyms; others speak of development only when they refer to underdeveloped countries or regions; others again want development to convey a connotation of fundamental changes in social attitudes and institutions. In any case, economic development *is* economic growth, and a discussion of economic growth includes the growth of developing economies. Of course, some of the things that have to be said in this essay have only limited applicability, either to the growth of advanced economies only or only to the growth of backward economies. This will usually be clear from the context.

Whatever measures or indices there are of educational growth and of economic growth, they regularly move together. For example, if we look at the statistics of a nation's total educational expenditures and of its aggregate income, we find that both figures increase year after year. But this says nothing about the train of causation. As a matter of fact, this train may run in both directions, though with different reliability and in different running time. Some kinds of educational effort lead to increased productivity and hence to higher national income, but usually it takes several years on the average for these effects to materialize. After all, it will be many years before the youngster now in first grade reaches the labor market and starts working; and many things that he is taught may contribute little or nothing to the efficiency of his work. The effects in the other direction, the effects of rising incomes upon outlays for education, are more certain and much faster. Diminishing poverty and increasing affluence allow larger expenditures for education, and the demand for education may rise as soon as incomes go up. Moreover, increases in income per head usually mean higher wages and salaries, and this causes the cost of education to rise relative to the cost of goods that are produced with increasing productivity.

INTRODUCTION

These preliminary considerations suggest that the following discussion be organized under three headings: I. The Productive Contribution of Education; II. The Increasing Demand for Education; and III. The Increasing Cost of Education.

I
The Productive Contribution of Education

Educational efforts may be regarded as consumption, investment, waste, or drag. They are consumption to the extent that they give immediate satisfaction to the pupil or student (e.g., the joy of learning) or to others (e.g., mothers and neighbors enjoying some peaceful hours while the youngsters are at school). They are investment to the extent that they create either future nonpecuniary satisfaction (e.g., the joy of reading and learned discourse) or future gains in productivity. They are waste to the extent that they contribute neither to pleasure nor to productivity.[1] They are a handicap, or drag, to the extent that they make workers' preferences and opportunities of employment incompatible.

Our present concern is with education promoting

1. Fritz Machlup, *The Production and Distribution of Knowledge in the United States* (Princeton, N.J.: Princeton University Press, 1962), pp. 108–10, 115.

productivity and economic growth. Hence, we must try to understand the processes by which such effects can be achieved.

Factors in Economic Growth

Increases in total national product—not counting leisure as a product—may be due to

1. the use of more labor
2. the use of more physical capital
3. the use of better labor
4. the use of better machines and
5. the more efficient allocation and use of labor, materials, and machines.

1. Since we are interested chiefly in the increase of national product *per head*, we must realize that the use of more labor will contribute to such an increase only if the ratio of working to nonworking people increases. This ratio depends on (*a*) the age composition of the population, (*b*) the labor-force-participation rate, (*c*) the employment rate, and (*d*) the length of the work week. Education may have some influence, positive or negative, on these factors. Think, for example, of the effects of compulsory schooling upon the relative numbers of children and women in the labor force—fewer working

children but more working mothers—or of the effects of improved education upon labor mobility and thereby upon the employment rate. In advanced countries the greatest positive effect is on the labor-force-participation rate: the percentage of people in the labor force increases with the number of years of school completed.

2. The use of more physical capital is to a large extent a question of the saving habits and investment propensities of the people. Education may have influence on both saving and investing, but the influence may as well be negative as positive. (For example, the propensity to consume may be raised.) In any case, the influence would be too subtle and too slow-working to be taken into account in the educational planning of a country.

3. It is with regard to the third factor, improvements in the quality of labor, that education can play a really significant role. Positive effects may be expected on five scores: (*a*) better working habits and discipline, increased labor efforts, and greater reliability; (*b*) better health through more wholesome and sanitary ways of living; (*c*) improved skills, better comprehension of working requirements, and increased efficiency; (*d*) prompter adaptability to momentary changes, especially in jobs which require quick evaluation of new information and, in general, fast reactions; and (*e*) increased

capability to move into more productive occupations when opportunities arise. All levels of education may contribute to improving the quality of labor.

4. To the use of better machines, education can contribute in at least two ways: (*a*) by making people more interested in improved equipment, more alert to its availability, and more capable of using it; and (*b*) by training people in science and technology and expanding their capacity for the research and development work needed to invent, develop, adapt, and install new machines.

5. More efficient allocation and use of labor, materials, and machines may be the result of developments that have nothing to do with education (for example, economies of scale) but also of some that can be significantly promoted by education. We may list the following avenues of approach: (*a*) technical progress not embodied in machines, but engineered by trained people; (*b*) abolition of restrictive measures by government or private groups (though one must admit that educated people have voted for the introduction of counterproductive restrictions as often as for their abolition); (*c*) improved organization and management; and (*d*) greater adaptability and mobility of labor, without which more efficient allocation would not be possible.

THE PRODUCTIVE CONTRIBUTION OF EDUCATION

Having seen, for each of the five factors that may account for economic growth, the kind of contribution possibly made by education, we turn to the question of whether these contributions to economic growth can be quantified.

Assessing the Contributions to Growth

Economists have become increasingly ambitious lately; they are no longer satisfied with theoretical speculations about the growth of national income and the factors that contribute to it, but want to measure these contributions. The propensity to obtain numerical measurements from statistical data has increased rapidly in recent years. Fifty years ago statistical data of national income were virtually nonexistent. Now we have them for most countries. It is sometimes forgotten, however, that the preparation of the data involves a good deal of artful juggling of ideas and figures that are, not the result of observation, but of invention, imaginative construction, and heroic guesswork.[2] Hence, the use of these statistical series for "measuring"

2. "The statistician who supposes that he can make a purely objective estimate of national income, not influenced by preconceptions concerning the 'facts,' is deluding himself; for whenever he includes one item or excludes another he is implicitly accepting some standard of judgment, his own or that of the compiler of his data.

exactly how much each of a variety of things has contributed to the "observed" growth of national income may strike some of the more cautious economists as excessive boldness. One should realize that nothing in modern economics is more speculative than quantitative empirical research. No one ought to be surprised, therefore, if the results obtained by different investigators differ rather widely.

Most appraisers of the various contributions to economic growth begin by finding out how much of the increase in national income during the last two or three decades may be attributed to *increments* in inputs and how much to *improvements in their quality and their use*. The income increase due to additional inputs is measured by holding the productivity of the inputs and the efficiency of their use constant, thus applying for the entire period the rate of earning (per person and per dollar value of physical capital) that prevailed in the base year, the beginning of the period. The part of national income of

---

There is no escaping this subjective element in the work, or freeing the results from its effects. In consequence, all national income estimates are appraisals of the end products of the economic system rather than colorless statements of fact; and, like all appraisals, they are pre-determined by criteria that are at worst a matter of chance, at best a matter of deliberate choice." Simon Kuznets, *National Income and Its Composition, 1919–1938* (New York: National Bureau of Economic Research, 1941), Vol. 1, p. 3.

THE PRODUCTIVE CONTRIBUTION OF EDUCATION

the end year that is not "explained" by increments in inputs of labor and capital is called the residual. This residual is attributed to "progress"; some analysts went no further, although by speaking of it as "technical progress" they may have given a wrong impression. Indeed, some advocates of more government support for research and development jumped to the conclusion that all of the residual could be credited to technological improvements and inventions.

Other analysts attempted to dissect the residual.[3] Some were satisfied with a separation of the part of technical progress that was "embodied" in improved capital goods—in machines of more recent "vintage"—from the part not so embodied, which (torturing the English language) they called "disembodied" progress, meaning more efficient processes of production and more efficient use of labor and capital. Other analysts preferred to exhibit more clearly the contribution of education. One of the methods, pioneered by T. W. Schultz, "explained" the largest part of the residual as the return to investment in an increased "stock of education." Attempts to divide the residual between the contribution of education through improvements in the quality of

3. The discussion of this dissection may be too technical for readers without some training in economics. They may prefer to skip the next three paragraphs.

labor and the contribution of technology through improvements of production processes and machinery led to very divergent estimates. The most detailed imputation of the residual, to almost two dozen different elements, was that by Edward Denison; it credited improvements in the quality of labor, due to increased education, for as much as 23 percent of the increase in real national income.[4] Another appraiser had arrived at only 5.3 percent as his assessment of this contribution.[5]

By offering a brief sketch of Schultz's approach,[6] we may give to uninitiated readers a better idea of some of the steps involved in this and similar investigations. Schultz compared the real income of the United States in 1929 and 1957 and calculated the portion of the increase that would not be "explained" by the increases in the labor force and in "nonhuman wealth" (physical

4. Edward F. Denison, *The Sources of Economic Growth in the United States and the Alternatives before Us*, Committee for Economic Development, Supplementary Paper no. 13, (New York, 1962); idem, "Measuring the Contribution of Education to Economic Growth," in E. A. G. Robinson and J. E. Vaizey, eds., *The Economics of Education* (London: Macmillan; New York: St. Martin's Press, 1966), p. 212.

5. Hector Correa, *The Economics of Human Resources* (Amsterdam: North-Holland Publishing Company, 1963), p. 172.

6. Theodore W. Schultz, "Education and Economic Growth," in Nelson B. Henry, ed., *Social Forces Influencing American Education*, Sixtieth Yearbook of the National Society for the Study of Education, pt. 2 (Chicago: University of Chicago Press, 1961), especially pp. 78–82.

capital plus land) at earnings per person and returns per dollar value of physical wealth equal to those of 1929. He found that $71 billion of the increase in income earned by labor (or $88.8 billion of the increase in income of labor and capital) was the "unexplained" residual. He then compared—and this was Schultz's original contribution—the "total value of the stock of education" in 1957 with that of 1930 and divided the increase of that stock into two parts: Part One is the increase that would have been required "to keep the stock of education per laborer constant" at its earlier level, that is, the part invested in the increased labor force to give each worker the average education of 1930; Part Two is the "stock of education added" by raising the educational level of the average worker. The return on this additional human capital can "explain," depending on the presumed rate of return, between 36 and 70 percent of the "otherwise unexplained increase" in labor income (and a little less of the increase in income of labor and physical capital combined).

Several serious objections can be raised against this approach. The basic idea, however, that much has been invested in education and that this investment must have yielded a return in the form of a faster growth of national income, is sound. Questionable are the numerical results. The amount of theorizing, based on excessively meager empirical evidence, that enters into the statistical estimates is too large to justify confidence in the quantitative findings. One of the objections seems to be valid for all approaches that try to explain the "residual unexplained by the increments in factor inputs": the size of this residual itself depends too much on the choice of the period, that is, on the years selected as the first and the last of the series. Remember that the "explained increase" is found by multiplying the increments in inputs by the rates of earning of the base year. Earnings per worker may perhaps be sufficiently stable (close to the trend line) to qualify for use in estimates of the "explained increase in labor income," but the rate of return on the value of physical capital is highly unstable and there is hardly a good justification for taking the rate of the base year for estimating the "explained increase in income from capital." One may also question the estimates of the values of physical capital regarded as inputs, especially if one realizes that the rate of utilization of equipment fluctuates widely. Should unused capacity be assumed to yield a return on its historical book value at some historical rate? Or, indeed, should it be assumed to yield any return at all?

Finally, Schultz's approach takes it for granted that the private rates of return earned on private investment in one's additional education, that is, in essence the additional incomes earned by the more educated compared with the incomes of those with fewer years of schooling, correspond to actual additions to real national income and are not merely matters of its distribution. The calculation of private returns on educational investment will be discussed later in detail.

To question the numerical findings of any of these investigations is not to cast doubt on the theory itself. The theory of the productive contribution of education remains plausible even if the attempts to measure the contribution have not had convincing results.

Education and Size of Labor Force

The previous discussion of the contribution of education to economic growth has emphasized the improvements in the quality of labor and capital and in the efficiency of their use. However, by taking the increments in inputs, particularly the increments in the supply and employment of labor, as given and seeking the productive contribution of education only in the residual (that is, in the rise in national income not explained by the increased inputs), one loses sight of the effect of education on the people's willingness to work. Education can be of considerable influence on labor-force participation and employment.

In industrially advanced countries this influence is usually positive and sometimes highly significant. In a recent study for the United States, educational attainment, measured by years of school completed, is shown to be strongly associated with labor-force participation, even after allowance has been made for the influence of certain control variables (age, marital status, color, other income).[7] This positive association was exhibited for the census weeks of three different years, 1940, 1950, and 1960. In 1960 the labor-force-participation rate of males between thirty-five and forty-four years old was 67.5 percent for those without schooling, 87.1 percent for those with one to four years of schooling, 91.4 percent for those with five to seven years of schooling, and so forth, rising to 98.7 percent for those with sixteen years of schooling. Although the precise numbers were different in the earlier years, their increases with the years of schooling were also remarkably regular.

It is not difficult to find a theoretical explanation of this positive association of labor-force participation with educational experience: as education raises the market value of labor, the cost of not working increases, and in advanced economies, the chance of obtaining a job

7. William G. Bowen and T. Aldrich Finegan, *The Economics of Labor Force Participation* (Princeton, N.J.: Princeton University Press, 1969), pp. 53–62.

improves. The expectation of getting a better job at better wages increases the willingness of the more educated to seek employment. Those with less education have less to lose by staying out of the labor force and, hence, more of them actually fail to "participate" (as the economists say in their jargon) in the labor force.[8]

Although we may chalk this up as a significant influence of education upon national product, we must be careful not to generalize. We have cautiously qualified the proposition by limiting its validity to industrially advanced countries. We shall see later that meaningful participation in the labor force and gainful employment may be negatively associated with educational attainment: this may be the case in economies which do not provide the job opportunities desired by persons who have become too educated to work as common laborers.

Education and Population Growth

It is generally recognized that excessive population growth may inhibit the growth of national product per head. We should ask, therefore, whether we can find significant links between education and changes in death rates and birth rates.

8. *Ibid.*, p. 53.

Drastic reductions in death rates may be regarded as results of the application of new knowledge in medicine and public health, and thus as indirect results of education. The effects of lower death rates on national income per head are, however, not so simple as one may think at first. If the death rate falls because of reduced infant mortality, population growth will usually be accelerated, with possibly harmful effects on income per head. (In exceptional societies, though, reductions in infant mortality may be associated with compensatory reductions in births.) If the death rate were to fall because of reduced mortality of adolescents or of adults of working age, the resulting growth in population might contribute to an increase, not a retardation, in income per head. A fall in the death rate because of greater longevity of retired old people would in general tend to increase the ratio of nonworking to working people and thus to retard the growth of income per head; conceivably this tendency could be partially offset if older women took care of their grandchildren, thereby allowing mothers to go to work. On balance, reductions in the death rate not compensated by reductions in the birth rate are likely to retard the growth of income per head.

In most countries, even less developed ones, the reduction in death rates is largely an accomplished fact. If the decline can be attributed to education, then past, not current, education has to be credited for producing the new knowledge which resulted in reduced mortality. We may therefore take the reduced death rates as given, and with them the danger of a population explosion if high birth rates continue. In these circumstances, reductions in birth rates would allow income per head to increase faster. And if education can help to bring birth rates down, one may credit it with another contribution to economic growth.

Perhaps we should briefly explain the favorable effects of reduced fertility upon income per head.[9] There are at least five such effects. First, fewer people have to share total output (which is initially unchanged, since the smaller number of births will not affect the labor force for twelve to fifteen years). Second, more capital may become available, since reduced family size increases the capacity to save, and larger savings permit better equipment per worker. Third, though the labor force after twelve to fifteen years will be smaller than it would be if fertility were undiminished, output per worker will as a rule be larger, with more capital and natural resources per worker. Fourth, the labor force will be healthier as a result of reduced malnutrition, since there will be fewer children to feed. Fifth, the

9. See, for example, George C. Zaidan, "Population Growth and Economic Development," *Finance and Development*, Vol. 6 (March 1969).

labor force may be better educated because of a better nutritional foundation in infancy and of fewer children to be taught.[10]

The importance of birth rates for the age composition of the population is easily comprehended. While developed countries with birth rates below 20 per 1,000 people have about 25 percent of their populations consisting of children under fifteen years old, less developed countries with birth rates of 40 per 1,000 have between 40 and 45 percent of their populations under the same age. A simple arithmetic model comparing two countries, one with reduced, the other with undiminished fertility, shows that the "standard of living in a country which reduced its fertility would be 40 percent higher than otherwise at the end of 30 years, and over twice as high at the end of 60 years."[11]

It now remains for us to show how education may affect the birth rate. It can do so (*a*) by providing a better understanding of the social implications of the population

10. According to a report of an International Conference on Malnutrition, Learning, and Behavior, millions of young children in developing countries are experiencing some degree of retardation in learning because of inadequate nutrition. Good nutrition during the first three years of life is particularly important. See N. S. Scrimshaw and E. Gordon, eds., *Malnutrition, Learning, and Behavior* (Cambridge, Mass.: Massachusetts Institute of Technology Press, 1968).

11. Zaidan, "Population Growth," p. 4.

explosion, by attenuating hostilities toward birth control, and by conveying information about effective methods of contraception; (*b*) by contributing in various ways to increases in incomes and thereby spurring the demand for leisure-time activities which can be better enjoyed without the encumbrance of excessively large families; (*c*) by increasing the cost of raising children if they have to be sent to school and cannot help their parents in the home and in the fields; and (*d*) by opening opportunities for occupations other than farming, in which children cannot help and may be a burden. The last two arguments, of course, refer only to the chiefly agricultural economies of developing regions.

Unproductive and Counterproductive Education

After surveying the various processes by which education can contribute to economic growth, it is hardly necessary to point out that surely not every kind of educational effort and expenditure can be credited with such effects. Whether they accelerate the growth of productivity will depend on what is taught and how, to whom and at what levels, in what proportions and under what conditions. The same methods or school curricula that are highly productive in one country may be counterproductive in another. And, of course, many educational services—subjects taught and methods used—have no effect, either positive or negative, upon productivity and are not designed for such a purpose.

Lest these statements be misunderstood, two warnings seem necessary. The first is to avoid too narrow an understanding of *productivity*. This word should not be interpreted as relating to physical output alone; our previous references to improvements in organization were not intended to be limited to organization of the technical processes of production but were to include all sorts of decision-making processes, including the political. Secondly, the utility of education should be recognized also when the productivity of the educated in the widest sense of the word (including their capacity to reason, to persuade, to inspire, to govern, and to make decisions) is not increased. In other words, education may be valuable even if it is not productive of anything but an enhanced appreciation of the good, the true, and the beautiful. Nevertheless, we must understand the solicitude of legislators and administrators in charge of appropriating scarce resources, wanting to show that most of the funds channeled into education are used not just for "luxuries" but for social investment yielding high returns to society.

It is not immediately clear why some educational efforts should have negative effects upon productivity.

THE PRODUCTIVE CONTRIBUTION OF EDUCATION

One or two examples, however, will show how education sometimes can be a hindrance instead of a help to economic efficiency. We have learned of the growth-retarding effects of primary education in chiefly agricultural societies where the "educated" refuse to work in agriculture but cannot be absorbed into industry. Similarly, it has often been observed that secondary and higher education may lead to aversion to manual work while opportunities for nonmanual work are lacking. As Sir Arthur Lewis has said, "An education system may very easily produce more educated people than the economic system can currently absorb in the types of jobs or at the rates of pay which the educated expect. . . . In the long run the educated learn to expect different jobs and to accept lower rates of pay. But the long run may be very long, and the jobs accepted may gain very little from the education received."[12] The transition period may be of agonizing length and may be characterized by distressing unemployment, poverty, and frustration. To be sure, the uneducated members of the family who stay on the farm are by no means well off

12. W. Arthur Lewis, "Education and Economic Development," *Social and Economic Studies* (Jamaica), Vol. 10 (1961); reprinted in *International Social Science Journal*, Vol. 14 (1962) (hereafter cited as *I.S.S.J.*); and in Mary Jean Bowman, et al., eds., *Readings in the Economics of Education* (Paris: UNESCO, 1968) (hereafter cited as *Readings*). The quotation is from *I.S.S.J.*, p. 686, and *Readings*, p. 136.

and the product of their labor may be meager, but those who have gone to school and away from home are now crowding the city slums, have no jobs, are miserable, and produce nothing except threats to political stability. In such circumstances education is a drag to economic development.

This is a very different story from that which some idealists have told us about the great blessings which more education bestows on a poor country. Alas, "the amount of education which 'pays for itself' in a poor country is limited."[13] "In most African territories less than 25 percent of children aged 6 to 14 are in school," and it would be too ambitious to aim at "a goal of 50 percent within ten years."[14] According to a recent press report, in Kano, one of the richest of the northern states of Nigeria, only about 50,000 children of a school-age population of 850,000, that is, 1 child out of every 17, or less than 6 percent, attend primary school.

Instead of aiming at social justice in providing schooling for all, a poor country does much better in having only one-fifth or even less of its children go to primary school, but providing secondary education for some of the more talented. To offer several additional years of

13. Lewis, *I.S.S.J.*, p. 686; *Readings*, p. 135.
14. Lewis, *I.S.S.J.*, p. 689; *Readings*, p. 138.

schooling for fewer children seems to be the optimum educational plan for the poorest countries.

To aim for large enrollment ratios in the lower grades is especially wasteful if the drop-out rate is very high. There is sufficient evidence for the judgment that only one year of schooling is completely worthless. Yet in Haiti in 1960 only one-sixth of those in first grade went to second grade, and only one-tenth to third grade. The situation is a little better in "semi-advanced" countries, to use the terminology of Fred Harbison and Charles Myers. In Mexico and Venezuela, for example, 15 percent of the children attending first grade stayed in school through the sixth grade; and in Chile 21 percent went that far.[15] It is difficult to say whether and how the waste of abortive first years could be avoided.

Secondary and vocational education for the most teachable graduates of primary school has paid off very well for most developing countries. Secondary schools produce the persons who, with some brief additional training, become "technologists, secretaries, nurses, school teachers, bookkeepers, clerks, civil servants, agricultural assistants and supervisory workers" and who make up "the middle and upper ranks of business."[16]

15. Frederick Harbison and Charles A. Myers, *Education, Manpower and Economic Growth* (New York: McGraw-Hill., 1964), p. 110.
16. Lewis, *I.S.S.J.*, p. 690; *Readings*, p. 138.

Higher education in very poor countries can be justified only on grounds other than as a contribution to economic growth, perhaps as satisfying national pride or creating a nucleus for cultural development. In some countries, such as Colombia, as many as one-half the graduates of the university cannot find any jobs in which their education could be used.[17] Most of them emigrate, and the large cost of their education is wasted from the point of view of the nation. Be it that the demand for top-level talent is inadequate in the underdeveloped economy or that the university offers the wrong type of education, in any case these poor countries would surely have much more productive uses for their scarce resources.[18]

This situation does not hold for all less developed countries. Where the universities stress scientific and

17. Theodore P. Schultz, *Returns to Education in 'Bogota, Colombia* (Santa Monica, Calif.: Rand Corporation, 1968), pp. 37–40.

18. This conclusion is strongly supported by the most recent study on India. Differential earnings yield much lower returns to college graduates than to primary-school leavers. This is so in spite of the fact that the bulk of the college graduates are employed in the public sector (and probably paid above their marginal private product), whereas the bulk of primary-school leavers are employed in the private sector. The conclusion, clearly, is that "higher education [in India] is overexpanded relative to primary education." Mark Blaug, Richard Layard, and Maureen Woodhall, *The Causes of Graduate Unemployment in India* (London: Allen Lane, Penguin Press, 1969), Ch. 10.

technical education and where the economies are sufficiently industrialized to absorb the university graduates, the case for institutions of higher education may be strong. However, in many of the less developed countries the majority of university students are enrolled in the humanities, fine arts, and law—courses of study that are unlikely to contribute to increases in productivity. In India, 58 percent of the students are in these fields. In Uruguay, only 6 per cent of the students are in scientific or technological departments. These countries may be contrasted with Czechoslovakia, where only 6 percent study humanities, fine arts, and law, and 46 percent are in scientific and technological fields.[19] Lest I be accused of gross materialism and anti-intellectualism, let me emphasize that nothing in my statements is intended to disparage the cultural value of the humanities and the fine arts. I am questioning only whether very poor countries can afford this kind of education while they have to stint on investments in human and physical capital with high rates of return.

Fast Pay-Off: Training on the Job and Adult Education

Even those types of school education that raise the productive capacity of their recipients have rather long

19. Harbison and Myers, *Education*, p. 115.

pay-off periods. This is true for all levels of schooling, but especially for elementary education, because several years must elapse before the pupil is old enough to become gainfully employed, and for some forms of higher education, chiefly because its high cost (largely in the form of income foregone during the years of study) can be repaid only by many years of increased earnings by the graduate. Thus, even if the rates of return on the investment are high in terms of life-term earnings, it takes a long time for the investment to pay for itself.

There is one type of education that may pay for itself within a brief period: training on the job.[20] Even this statement does not hold if the term is interpreted so widely that it includes all kinds of learning on the job. We ought to distinguish three forms of education on the job (or "in service"): (1) training programs provided by business firms using an instructing staff for employees (inclusive of management personnel) newly hired or reassigned; (2) informal training by firms, without the use of instructors, to break in the new man, under the supervision of a foreman or older workers, as he performs his new tasks with increasing speed and accuracy; and (3) informal learning by a worker trying to improve his performance and skill in order·to become eligible for advancement to higher pay or a better job.

20. Machlup, *Production and Distribution*, pp. 57–64.

THE PRODUCTIVE CONTRIBUTION OF EDUCATION

Learning on the job is not paid for by an employer nor guided by a supervisor; it may be employment in a "growth job," that is, a job paying little to beginners but holding out the chance of much higher incomes for those who become efficient. In such cases, the investment period may be quite long. In the first two cases, however, training on the job may return its cost very quickly. This is especially likely where the employer pays for the training without having any assurance that the worker will stay with him. In view of the risk of losing the trained workers before long, employers will have a strong incentive to choose training methods and employee assignments that have a quick pay-off.

Since brief pay-off periods are especially important where capital is in short supply, training on the job recommends itself to poor countries. Hence the wise counsel by an expert adviser on economic development:

> The quickest way to increase productivity in the less developed countries is to train the adults who are already on the job. Education for children is fine, but its potential contribution to output over ten years is small compared with the potential contribution of efforts devoted to improving adult skills.[21]

This statement links on-the-job training provided by employers with adult education sponsored by public or civic agencies. While the return is probably slower and

21. Lewis, *I.S.S.J.*, p. 693; *Readings*, p. 141.

less certain for adult education than for training on the job, it will probably be much faster than for primary-school education. After completion of evening classes, vocational-training and agricultural-extension programs, and similar kinds of adult education, the upgraded adult may without delay be fit for an employment that makes use of the newly acquired skills. However, if programs of adult education are to succeed, it will be necessary to arouse popular enthusiasm for learning. People do not learn against their will; it takes a degree of commitment and passion for people to make the required effort. If a "mass movement" for adult education can be stirred up, the rate of return on this investment may be much higher than that on other educational outlays.

Private and Social Returns

Can we really know the rates of return on investment in various kinds of education, by different methods, in different subjects, and on different levels? In recent years much work has been done on these problems. Numerical estimates of returns on educational investment have been made for many countries, developing as well as developed. These estimates have been based on statistical information, some good, some bad; on hypothetical assumptions, some plausible, some rather implausible; on theoretical reasoning, some sound, some questionable; and on computations, some elementary, some quite sophisticated. To get an idea of the principles involved, one must first acquaint oneself with the essential concepts.

Rates of return are calculated by comparing a stream of incomes or benefits with a stream of outlays or costs. The costs and the benefits may be merely *private*, that is, those incurred by or accruing to the individual recipient of education (or his parents); or they may be *social*, that is, they may include, over and above the private costs and benefits, those incurred by or accruing to third persons and society at large.

Private costs are partly explicit, for example, money outlays for tuition fees or expenditures for books, stationery, and transportation; and partly implicit, chiefly the earnings foregone by older students who could have taken jobs instead of going to school.

Social costs include, in addition to all private costs, the capital cost and operating expenses of public schools and universities, and the various subsidies, stipends, and grants from governments and from philanthropic individuals, corporations, and foundations, as well as some implicit costs of the government, for example, tax revenues foregone because of exemptions from real-property taxation or because of the loss of income taxes on the earnings which students sacrificed by going to school.

The benefits from education are partly pecuniary and partly nonpecuniary. Private pecuniary benefits consist of the increments in earnings that are attributable to additional years of education. (The basic data required are the incomes earned by persons with different amounts and levels of education. If all other factors that may account for differences in earnings can be properly evaluated, one may obtain the differential earnings that can reasonably be attributed to different amounts and types of education.) Private nonpecuniary benefits consist of the various satisfactions which the student (or his family) possibly derives, at the time, from his school attendance and, in later years, from the education received in the past. (Since appraisals of money equivalents of such "psychic incomes" would be entirely subjective on the part of the individuals and not ascertainable by any statistical-census taker, nonpecuniary benefits are omitted from estimates of returns on educational investment.)

Social benefits from education, as usually conceived, include, in addition to the private benefits (that is, chiefly the differential earnings of the educated to the extent that they reflect additions to and not merely redistributions of national income), any benefits that accrue to third parties and to society at large. Third-party benefits and most of those to society cannot be estimated, however; only one factor, the contribution of education to technological progress, is sometimes assessed as an additional element in the social benefits of education.

Readers to whom these conceptual distinctions are new may find it convenient to have them reinforced by a line-by-line summary, enumerating four items of costs of education and four items of benefits from education:

- A. Explicit costs incurred by students or their families (money outlays)
- B. Implicit costs incurred by students or their families (chiefly earnings foregone)
- C. Explicit costs incurred by third parties or the public (money outlays)
- D. Implicit costs incurred by third parties or the public (chiefly earnings or tax revenues foregone)

- E. Pecuniary benefits accruing to the educated or their families (earnings in money or in kind)
- F. Nonpecuniary benefits accruing to the educated or their families (satisfactions, psychic incomes)
- G. Pecuniary benefits accruing to third parties or the public (money incomes or tax revenues)
- H. Nonpecuniary benefits accruing to third parties or the public (satisfactions, psychic incomes)

Items *A* and *B* together are the private costs; items *A*, *B*, *C*, and *D* together are the social costs.

Items *E* and *F* together are the private benefits; items *E*, *F*, *G*, and *H* together are the social benefits.

Private benefits minus private costs are private net benefits, or net returns. Social benefits minus social costs are social net benefits, or net returns. The rate of return is calculated by finding the rate of discount (capitalization) that equates the capitalized value (present value) of the stream of benefits with the capitalized value of the stream of costs.[22]

Differences in Private Incomes and National Product

The strategic item in any discussion of the returns on investment in education is *E*, the pecuniary benefits

22. The customary exclusion of nonpecuniary (positive or negative) benefits is chiefly a matter of avoiding the arbitrary appraisals that would have to be made in the absence of information about the subjective valuations by all the individuals concerned. Even if one entertained the fiction that all individual valuations of satisfactions and dissatisfactions were becoming known to an imaginary cost-benefit analyst, the analyst would have to exclude all dissatisfactions that are caused by envy of the fortunes of luckier persons and by pity for the misfortunes of unluckier ones, and exclude likewise all feelings of satisfaction about the good fortunes of friends and about the misfortunes of enemies. This remark serves merely as a safeguard against possible misunderstandings regarding the role of psychic

accruing to the educated. These benefits are understood as the additional lifetime earnings that can be attributed to additional education. The question is, additional to what? The answer at first seems simple: additional to something less, perhaps additional to that lower level of education at which a less eager student may have stopped. In line with the idea that education is an investment in one's earning capacity, we may perhaps answer: additional to that level of education beyond which a rational person may be considering going as a prudent investor in greater earning capacity. The rational college graduate who considers going to graduate school asks what additional income the average holder of an M.A. degree can earn over and above the income of one who has a B.A. and what further addition a Ph.D. holder can earn above the income of a graduate with an M.A. The rational high-school graduate compares the earnings of college graduates with those of people without college education, and a high-school student who considers dropping out after his junior year will, if he is rational, ask how large the difference is between the earnings of a high-school graduate and the earnings of a person with only eleven

---

incomes in cost-benefit analyses, for, if double counting or cancellations of increases in the incomes of some persons or groups are to be avoided, psychic incomes must not include the joys and heartaches about the affluence or poverty of other people.

years of schooling. If we now skip to the low end of the educational ladder, the rational parents of a child approaching school age will ask what difference it would make for his future income if he does or does not go to elementary school.

For the private rate of return on educational investment, this simulation of rational considerations makes good sense; and the statistical findings about the incremental earnings that can, after evaluation of all other differentiating factors, be attributed to additional education may be recognized as measures of the essential pecuniary benefits accruing to the recipients of the added years of education in question. One must ask, however, whether these same differentials in the earnings of the recipients of different amounts of education can be legitimately used for the determination of the social returns. For it is conceivable that the incremental earnings of the group with more education neither represent additions to national product nor reflect the magnitude of such additions.[23]

Assume a society in which all workers have had nine years of schooling; a certain percentage of the people now extend their education to twelve years. If, after they enter the labor force they earn more than those with only

23. Mary Jean Bowman, "Social Returns to Education," *International Social Science Journal* (UNESCO), Vol. 14 (1962), pp. 656–57.

nine years, the difference in incomes will measure the addition to the aggregate product only if the income of those with only nine years of schooling has not changed in the process. Perhaps, however, the availability of more highly qualified labor has raised the productivity of the less qualified; this will be the case if a large degree of complementarity exists between the two types of labor. That is to say, the cooperation of those with superior skills increases the productive efficiency of the less skilled workers. Thus, the difference in the incomes of the two groups will understate the increase in national product that results from the added education. Perhaps, on the other hand, the opposite condition prevails and the two types of labor are essentially competitive. If so, the new supply of superior labor will have reduced the demand for and consequently the income of the less qualified labor; in this case the income differential will overstate the contribution of the added education to national product.

In an extreme case there may be a large income differential between the two groups without there being any addition to national product. Assume that the additional education makes its recipients no more efficient but nevertheless more desirable to employers.[24] Incomes

24. The employee with more schooling but no greater efficiency may be more desirable to the employer because (a) the supervisors

of the less educated will decline as a result of the availability of the more favored and better-paid group. The private rate of return on the investment in additional education, then, may be high while the social rate is zero. Real national income is unchanged; only its distribution is altered. The pay-off to those who have invested in three more years of education may be satisfactory, but from the point of view of society the additional cost of education may be sheer waste, at least as long as material product is taken as the sole criterion of social productivity.

The conceptual scheme of social costs and benefits is equipped to take account of all such divergences between social and private returns. Item G of the list could reflect the divergences, for, in these instances, positive or negative pecuniary benefits accrue to third parties. As the group with additional schooling is absorbed into the economy and receives pecuniary benefits attributable to investment in its education, those with less education have their incomes increased or reduced, as the case may be. The trouble with the usual computations of social rates of return is that these third-party

---

enjoy the company of more educated workers, (b) the management gains prestige and greater consumer loyalty, and/or (c) the personnel office takes school certificates as less expensive substitutes for its own tests and evaluations. The third explanation is the most plausible.

effects are not observable and cannot be estimated by means of the statistical techniques at our disposal.

The analysts of the returns to education have not shown serious concern about these problems. Whether their sanguine confidence is justified is difficult to judge. Let us note the problem and proceed.

Isolating the Effects of Education

In speaking of income differentials attributable to additional education, one implicitly assumes that it is possible to separate the effects of various factors that may be responsible for differences in incomes. It would surely not be legitimate to disregard all other factors and to say that the full difference between the incomes of, say, college graduates and high-school graduates must be the result of college education and of nothing else.

The groups with different amounts of schooling or different kinds of education may differ in many other respects, for example, in age composition, and one must attempt to estimate the effects of the most evident of these differences upon income. Some factors—age, sex, color, ethnic origin, urban versus rural upbringing, years of work experience—are relatively easy to separate because they are among the census data, at least in some countries. We know that incomes increase with age (at least, up to a certain age); if the group of college graduates is younger than the group of high-school graduates, the income differential would understate the effect of college education; such a differential would overstate this effect if the group is older.

Other factors are more difficult to deal with. Take, for example, differences in incomes that are due to family background and connections with influential persons. (The son of a doctor or of a banker may get a better job than the son of a factory worker.) This factor may to some extent be estimated by using the income and the educational background of the father as separate variables.

The most complex problem is the separation of *native* ability, industry, and drive from *improvements* in skills and attitudes acquired through education. The greater earning capacity of college graduates, compared with high-school graduates, is, no doubt, to a large extent the result of superior native intelligence and greater ambition; it would be quite wrong to attribute all of the incremental earnings to the investment in college education. (The average intelligence quotient, I.Q., of college graduates is 120, while that of high-school graduates is only 107.) Some of the appraisers of the benefits from education have used rough rules of thumb:

THE PRODUCTIVE CONTRIBUTION OF EDUCATION

Denison, for example, assumed that two-fifths of the income differentials of persons with more schooling were due to their natural ability, energy, and similar personal qualities, while three-fifths were a result of their additional schooling.[25] Other analysts have tried to measure native ability and motivation by the students' class ranks and found that this accounted for one-fourth of the income differentials.[26] The most painstaking analysis was made by Becker.[27] He found samples of persons for whom intelligence quotients and grades in primary school were given, besides their incomes, schooling, and all the rest. Using the I.Q.'s for native ability and the grades in primary school for drive and ambition, he extracted the residual income differential that could with good conscience be attributed to additional formal education.

There is still another factor that is difficult to disentangle from the rest, namely, effects of that kind of informal learning on the job that is, not simply a function of years of experience, but depends on the type of learner and on the type of job—where, for example, the educational investment takes the form of foregoing a higher

25. Denison, "Measuring the Contribution of Education," p. 207.
26. Dael Wolfle and Joseph Smith, "The Occupational Value of Education for Superior High-School Graduates," *Journal of Higher Education*, Vol. 27 (April 1956), pp. 201–13.
27. Gary S. Becker, *Human Capital* (New York: Columbia University Press, 1964).

beginner's salary in the hope of faster advancement. The usual statistical techniques, which quantify formal education in terms of years of schooling (or perhaps in terms of "equivalent years," corrected for differences in the number of school days per year), cannot take account of the informal in-service learning in a growth job.

The theoretical insight that "increases in productivity with age [indicating work-experience] are more pronounced, and declines are less pronounced, in jobs requiring greater amounts of training" is generally supported by empirical studies showing strong correlation between "occupational ranks" and dispersion of incomes within each occupation.[28] The relevant occupational ranking is determined according to average earnings, which are taken as indicators of the amount of training required. One may find it intellectually satisfying to see the theory that "education pays" confirmed also for the case of informal learning from experience in occupations requiring higher skills. Yet one may at the same time regret that the difficulties of measurement and the consequent disregard of this educational investment may distort the estimates of rates of return on formal education.

28. Jacob Mincer, "Investment in Human Capital and Personal Income Distribution," *Journal of Political Economy*, Vol. 66 (August 1958), pp. 298–301.

THE PRODUCTIVE CONTRIBUTION OF EDUCATION

The Findings

Now what rates of return on the investment in incremental education have been found? Becker used several census years (1939, 1949, 1956, and 1958) in his calculations for the United States; his results from the different sets of data were of course not quite the same but were similar enough to give us some confidence in their order of magnitude. The private rates of return, before accounting for differences in native qualities, were quite stable for college education: for the four different sets of data, the rates were between 12.4 and 14.8 percent per annum.[29] Thus, an investment in four years of college yielded over the average working life of the graduate an annual return of about 13 percent. We must not forget, however, that the differential earnings become positive only after several years. Ten years after graduation the rate of return is still negative.[30] The 13 percent refers to life earnings.

The rates of return on high-school education in the United States were rising over the years, from 16 percent in 1939 to 28 percent in 1958. There are two explanations

29. Somewhat lower rates of return were calculated in a more recent analysis of data for 1959, using different estimating procedures for sorting out the effects of extraneous factors on personal earnings. See Giora Hanoch, "An Economic Analysis of Earnings and Schooling," *Journal of Human Resources*, Vol. 2 (Summer 1967), pp. 310–29.

30. Becker, *Human Capital*, p. 112.

for this increase. For the first one we have to remember that the returns compare earnings of high-school graduates with earnings of persons with only nine years of school, and the rates of return were calculated before taking account of native ability. We know that the percentage of youngsters completing the twelfth grade has much increased since 1939, so that now practically only the least talented, least motivated, and most handicapped fail to go to high school.[31] It stands to reason, therefore, that much of the differential earnings is really due to differences in native ability, not to high-school education as such. The second factor is probably the notorious shift in the demand for labor away from less skilled to better educated. Less educated persons are becoming unemployable at the minimum wages imposed by legislation, trade unions, and modern business ethics and prestige considerations. High-school education is becoming a condition of employment even where it contributes little to the skills required for the jobs in question.

The preceding remarks relate to the situation in the United States, and the figures reported are the *private* rates of return to education. Similar calculations have been made for many other countries, though the statistical bases were much weaker. A few of the findings may

31. *Ibid.*, p. 129.

be summarized here. A recent study of Bogota, Colombia, calculated semiprivate, or "partially social," rates of return. Partially social means that the costs to the government were added to the costs to the students and their families, but the benefits included no additional benefits to society over and above the income differentials earned by the educated. The reported partially social rates of return for men in Bogota were only 15 percent per annum for primary education, but 27 percent for secondary education and 35 percent for vocational training, yet only 3 percent for higher education. The returns were rather different for women: a zero rate of return for primary education, 14 percent for secondary school, 40 percent for vocational training, and 4 percent for university.[32] The zero return for primary school indicates that women without any schooling were getting the same kinds of jobs as women with several years of school. The 40 percent obtained on investment in vocational training was probably a result of the foreign-language skills acquired by typists and secretaries.[33] The extremely low rate of return reported for higher education, 3 percent for men, is still too high if social costs are correctly counted, since the calculation disregarded the loss of half the graduates through emigration. The private

32. Schultz, *Returns to Education*, p. 36.
33. *Ibid.*, p. 29.

rates of return for university education are probably much higher since the emigrants' earnings abroad, especially in the United States, greatly exceed the earnings of graduates in the home country.

In more developed countries the partially social rates of return from higher education are higher: 12 percent in Chile[34] and 20 percent in Venezuela.[35] In Mexico the private rate of return from higher education was found to be 40 percent.[36] For India, on the other hand, the social rate of return to education in general for men was reported to be less than 16 percent, and for secondary education alone was no more than 10 or 12 percent.[37] A more recent and more detailed study, on the basis of 1961 data, shows social rates for primary education as low as 13.7 percent, for secondary education 12.4 percent, and for college education 7.4 percent. The private rate

34. Arnold Harberger and Marcelo Selowsky, *Key Factors in Economic Growth in Chile*, mimeographed (Chicago, Ill., 1966).

35. Carl Shoup, *The Fiscal System of Venezuela* (Baltimore: Johns Hopkins Press, 1959).

36. Martin Cornoy, "Rates of Return to Schooling in Latin America," *Journal of Human Resources*, Vol. 2 (Summer 1967), p. 368, Table 7.

37. Arnold C. Harberger, "Investment in Men versus Investment in Machines: The Case of India," in C. Arnold Anderson and Mary Jean Bowman, eds., *Education and Economic Development* (Chicago: Aldine, 1965); A. M. Nalla Gounden, "Investment in Education in India," *Journal of Human Resources*, Vol. 2 (Summer 1967), p. 352, Table 2.

of return to the college graduate, compared with the illiterate, was only 15.2 percent, and the social rate 12.3 percent.[38] The author of one of the Indian studies reminds us of the very high rates of return on investment in physical capital (machines): they were between 17 and 26 percent, much higher than the yields from human capital.[39]

Working Hours and Leisure Time

I want to call attention to a question usually disregarded in the calculations and also in most discussions of the returns on investment in education—the question of changes in the allocation of time between work and leisure. If differences in the earnings of persons with different amounts of education are computed on an annual basis, we implicitly attach zero values to the pleasures derived from different types of work and from leisure. Assume, for purposes of illustration, that the average annual income of persons with only primary school is four thousand dollars; of those with secondary school, eight thousand dollars; and of those with college, twelve thousand dollars. Assume further, to make it simpler, that native intelligence and industry are the

38. Blaug, Layard, and Woodhall, *Causes of Graduate Unemployment in India*, Table 10.1.

39. Harberger, "Investment in Men," p. 29.

same for all three groups but that the first group works forty-eight hours a week; the second, forty hours; and the third, sixty hours. Does it make better sense to compare annual earnings or hourly earnings?

There are arguments for both procedures. The higher earnings of the college graduates would be due to their working one hour and a half for each hour worked by high-school graduates. The difference in hourly earnings is therefore nil. This would argue strongly against using annual earnings. On the other hand, perhaps the kind of work done by the college graduates is so enjoyable that they *want* to work more hours; they get more pleasure from working than from alternative uses of their time. This would argue against using hourly earnings; the difference (or absence of difference) in money earnings would underestimate the psychic-income differential.

This problem has no unique solution. Not even if we knew the preference maps of all individuals would we be equipped for a meaningful exercise in welfare economics, for, more likely than not, the individuals' preferences may be changed, along with their skills, by their additional education.[40] If the elasticities of substi-

---

40. I must apologize to the noneconomists among my readers: I realize that this and the next sentence will make hardly any sense to them, but to translate them into nontechnical language would take more time and space than can be justified by the importance of the problem.

tution between work and leisure are altered in the process of education, how can we evaluate the change in additional psychic income, particularly if more leisure time gave additional satisfaction before the change in tastes but reduced satisfaction after the change?

We must be satisfied with recognizing the existence of this question, for we are not able to do much about answering it.[41]

Additional Social Benefits

I have mentioned several times that most calculations confine themselves to only one kind of benefit, the differential earnings due to additional education, that is, incomes which, apart from taxes collected, accrue to the educated themselves. Undoubtedly, there are also many

---

41. The assumption of longer hours being worked by more educated people, although it was made here only for the sake of illustration, does to some extent correspond with observation. Approximately one more year of school was found to be associated with one more hour per week worked. See T. Aldrich Finegan, "Hours of Work in the United States: A Cross-Sectional Analysis," *Journal of Political Economy*, Vol. 70 (October 1962), p. 460. The positive correlation between hours of work and years of education may have several explanations: for example, college graduates may have acquired a taste for more work, or people with such taste are more likely to go to college, or more qualified work requires larger work loads.

nonpecuniary benefits accruing to the educated, and many accruing to third parties and to society at large. To assign particular money values to these nonpecuniary benefits would be too arbitrary and, hence, they are omitted from the calculation of returns from education.

Such omissions are often severely criticized. Let us sample at least one vote of censure:

Are not increased literacy, responsible participation in society and in politics, identification with national goals, improvement in physical and mental health, and development of attitudes and values favorable to progress just as important as national income and industrial productivity? May not the ultimate economic return of such results be more significant than the immediate gains in productivity? If so, how do we really measure the economic benefit of education? I distrust the manpower need approach as an adequate basis for educational planning. I equally distrust the increased earnings of the educated as a basis for measuring the values of education. The residual approach, so far as I understand it, seems to me to involve so many unknowns that it is not really informative.[42]

These strictures lump together too many different sins of omission and commission. There are perhaps good reasons for distrusting school-planning techniques designed to meet specific manpower needs; most of these

42. Paul L. Dressel, "Comments on the Use of Mathematical Models in Educational Planning" in Organisation for Economic Cooperation and Development, *Mathematical Models in Educational Planning* (Paris: OECD, Directorate for Scientific Affairs, 1967), p. 281.

THE PRODUCTIVE CONTRIBUTION OF EDUCATION

techniques apply input-output analysis to calculate the educational inputs required for an allegedly "needed" output of particular occupational skills.[43] There would also be strong reasons for distrusting the calculation of differential earnings if it were really used "as a basis for measuring the values of education." However, the analysts of private or social returns to education have repeatedly stressed that they were not estimating *all* the benefits from education but were omitting from their estimates of yields all those that cannot be quantified except by purely subjective valuation. The critic's complaint about there being too many unknowns in the regression analysis to allow disentangling the contribution education has made to the observed differences in earnings is understandable, but some ingenious analysts have succeeded in substituting measurable proxy variables for unknown ones and in presenting acceptable approximations to the wanted information.[44]

43. Jan Tinbergen et al., *Econometric Models of Education* (Paris: OECD, 1965).
44. This is not a defense of the subtleties paraded by the builders of mathematical models for educational planning. In order to understand all the essays included in *Mathematical Models in Educational Planning* (1967) the reader needs to know matrix algebra, linear programming, input-output analysis, the theory of absorbing Markov chains, and Pontryagin's maximum principle. See Mark Blaug, "Educational Planning: Review Article," *Minerva*, Vol. 6 (Autumn 1967), p. 44.

EDUCATION AND ECONOMIC GROWTH

There is, besides all the nonmeasurable benefits from education, at least one element in the growth of national income that is closely linked with education and can be to some extent statistically estimated: the part of economic growth that is attributable to the growth of knowledge, or the particular type of knowledge that allows greater efficiency in the use of labor, land, and capital.

We must first ask ourselves whether this contribution to economic growth is really additional to the contribution which education makes to the incremental earnings of educated individuals. Is there no double counting involved? That, in general, the two effects are different may be seen from a simple mental experiment: assume that there is no increase in the level of knowledge and that, with average productivity unchanged, average national income per head does not increase over time. There would still be income differentials, and the better educated would still earn more than the less educated. It is usually assumed that earnings reflect the income-earners' contributions to private profits (net revenues) and that these in turn reflect the respective contributions to national income. (These assumptions presuppose a sufficient degree of competition in all markets for products and productive factors, but they underlie all statistical estimates of rates of social return on investment

THE PRODUCTIVE CONTRIBUTION OF EDUCATION

in education.) The differential earnings in a stationary economy would still be relevant for the problem of estimating the social benefits from education, provided one can assume that it was differential education that was responsible for differential earnings. Now, if education produces not only differences in individual capacities but also new knowledge resulting in continuous technological, managerial, and organizational improvements, the growth in national product due to these improvements can reasonably be regarded as an additional contribution of education. The "structure" of earnings, that is, differences in earnings of groups with different amounts of education, is not the same thing as annual increases in the level of most earnings. From this point of view, the suspicion of double counting may be rejected as unfounded, and in estimating the social rate of return on investment in education, the nonprivate benefits from technological progress may be added to the private benefits from differential education.

One qualification to this verdict may be in order. Assume that a large number of persons in the group with many years of education are engaged in research and development, or in technical and managerial jobs, and their usefulness to the firms or agencies that employ them consists largely in the productive innovations they propose or introduce. The differential earnings of this educated group will then in large part be determined by their contribution to the growth of productive knowledge. Double counting would be involved after all. One may perhaps adjust for it by not adding to the private benefits the *full* contribution to the growth of productive knowledge as a nonprivate benefit from education.

If most or all of the growth of knowledge that leads to growing productivity of the economy is attributed to education, it goes without saying that we must not allow it to be attributed at the same time to research and development. One may, of course, engage in speculation about the comparative values of alternative uses of highly educated people; one may ask whether these persons may contribute to society more as managers, researchers, developers, teachers, politicians, and so forth; and one may hold that the existing allocation of these scarce resources is or is not optimal for society. In such speculation it may make sense to attempt separate estimates of the rates of return on investment in research and development. But since the same resources can be allocated only to one use at a time, the potential contribution of education will be measured by the optimal use made of the products of education, whether this is in research and development or in any other activity. If estimates of social rates of return are to serve government decisions about educational

THE PRODUCTIVE CONTRIBUTION OF EDUCATION

policies, then one is justified in counting among the social contributions of education the growth of productivity that rests on the production of new knowledge.

It will be remembered that Becker's estimates of the private rate of return on investment in college education in the United States centered at about 13 percent per annum. Becker gave us also an estimate of a social rate of return that included the growth of productivity as a nonprivate contribution of education. It came to about 25 percent per annum.[45] While the private rate of return is not particularly attractive relative to investment in physical capital, a social rate of return of the magnitude of Becker's estimate would be quite respectable, at least for the United States.

Several writers on the social benefits from education have pointed to another contribution of education, one that could not be measured but should nevertheless be regarded as of great importance to society: the effect of education on social and political stability. It has been taken for granted that education would increase the respect for law and order and promote a climate conducive to peaceful social, political, and economic development. The experience of the last few years, with student riots and rebellions at universities all over the world, may lead to a reconsideration of this assumption. It may

45. Becker, *Human Capital*, p. 120.

well be that the theory of the stabilizing and evolutionary-nonrevolutionary influence of education is pertinent only for a state of affairs in which access to higher education is confined to an elite with a strong interest in perpetuating its position in society. As the percentage of the population with twelve and sixteen years of education increases, the influence of education on political stability may well become negative. This remark, however, may be no more than idle speculation, induced by experiences too recent to be analyzed with sufficient historical perspective.

Rates of Return Calculated for Soviet Russia

I cannot refrain from reporting on studies made by Soviet economists about the productivity of education in Soviet Russia. Pioneering work in this field was undertaken by Stanislav G. Strumilin and first published about 1924. His work is fascinating for several reasons. First, his attempt to measure the economic, private and social, benefits from education preceded similar work in "bourgeois" economies by several years (if one may disregard the modest and largely forgotten anticipations by von Thünen and other early precursors). Second, the formulation of the benefits in terms of "profit," "productivity," and "rates of return on investment" is in remarkable contrast to Marxist terminology. Third, the assumption that a worker produces a "surplus product" that is not paid to him but accrues to society is an interesting reflection upon "socialist exploitation" analogous to "capitalist exploitation" presumably abolished.

Strumilin sets out to answer the question "what level of school qualification and what school expenditure per worker is most profitable" to the nation.[46] "To reach a rational solution of the problem of the optimum periods of school education for workers, a determination must be made of what each extra year of instruction gives the worker and the State, and how much it costs the worker's family and the State as a whole." He proceeds to calculate the yields, in wage differentials, of each additional year of schooling. But

the point is that the worker, by the product of his labor creates not only the value of his earnings but also an additional product for society. The surplus product, which increases with the rise in labour productivity and the worker's qualification, amounted before the Revolution to not less than 100% of his earnings, at the most modest estimate. Hence, the significance of the school for the income side of the State budget should be roughly double.

46. All quotations are from V. E. Komarov, "The Significance of Education: Excerpts from Socialist Writings," in Mary Jean Bowman et al., eds., *Readings*, pp. 61–62.

Strumilin then compares expenditures for education with "profits" from education:

> As can be seen, the profits accruing from the increase in labour productivity are 27.6 times greater [over the working life of the worker] than the corresponding outlay by the State on school education; this capital outlay from the exchequer is already repaid with interest during the first $1\frac{1}{2}$ years, while during the following $35\frac{1}{2}$ years the State receives an annual net income from this "capital" without any expenditure whatsoever. A more profitable investment of "capital" could hardly be imagined, even in countries with such extraordinary possibilities as Soviet Russia. And even so, we have still not taken into account the profits accruing, in the process, to the worker who raises his qualifications.

Reviewing the Soviet's investment in education for all children between six and twelve years of age, Strumilin concludes that

> the capital expenditure even towards the end of the first decade was repaid with interest by the corresponding increase in the national income, while the profitability of the expenditure for the following three decades exceeds 125% a year. And only during the first 5–6 years of its implementation is the financial burden of the reform on the country palpable.... Every Soviet worker playing a part in the production of material goods not only completely offsets the expenditure on the reproduction of his labour power but also creates a surplus product "for society" which can be used for social consumption and accumulation. The improvement in the level of workers' qualifications results not only in higher remuneration for their

THE PRODUCTIVE CONTRIBUTION OF EDUCATION

labour but also in an increase in their "social" product, which goes into the country's reserves for public consumption and accumulation. In studying the efficiency of school education and the profitability of investments in this field, therefore, account must also be taken of the portion of the surplus product resulting from improvement in the level of workers' qualifications.

Strumilin's idea that each worker "produces" much more than the wage he is paid—that he produces twice his wage—derives from Marx's theory of capitalist exploitation. If labor is regarded as the sole factor of production, any part of the national product that is not paid to the worker may be seen as "surplus value" appropriated by the employer. In the Soviet economy, the State is the employer "reaping" the surplus product. This theory has joined the assumption that labor is the sole productive service to the fact that the national product exceeds total wages; it has provided an effective argument to the propaganda against a system of exploitation that withholds from the worker a large part of "his" product.

Once it is conceded that there are other productive factors besides labor, the distribution of the total product can no longer be explained by the simple contention of one factor's being exploited by others. The product of a worker is measured by the difference which his participation in the process of production makes for the national output. If, with the existing capital equipment, given inventories, and available natural resources, the labor force is increased or reduced by one worker, the resulting increment or decrement of aggregate output is all that society can pay as wages to that last man. Of course, every worker is the last man when it comes to evaluating his productive contribution; and if there is a competitive arrangement in operation by which different employers offer their products and bid for productive factors, the wage paid to the worker will be no more and no less than the marginal product. No surplus product will be left for the employer, private or public, if competition is effective. The only exceptions are third-party benefits of the type discussed before. In the case of improvements in the efficiency of labor, the extra benefits that may accrue to others than the upgraded workers themselves are such things as the fruits of technological progress or the cultural, social, and (perhaps) political by-products of a better educated society.

Strumilin has continued to study and write about the economics of education. His more recent calculations of the returns on investment in education no longer rest on the educated workers' "surplus product" in excess of their wages. Instead, they are based on attributing increases in national income to three factors: increases in the labor force, increases in physical capital, and, as

THE PRODUCTIVE CONTRIBUTION OF EDUCATION

a residual, improvements in the quality of labor, the latter being regarded as the result of education. For 1960 he concluded that 23 percent of the national income of the Soviet Union could be imputed " to improvement in the qualifications of the labour force."[47] And over the twenty years, 1940 to 1960, he found that

> the addition to the national income due to higher and secondary education increased more than sixfold, and the net income, after deduction of current expenditure, increased tenfold. The average returns—for the national economy as a whole—from investments in this sector of cultural development has thus broken all known records, increasing from 52 to 144 per cent per annum.[48]

This figure seems fantastically high. However, I shall not undertake to check either his methods of calculation or the accuracy of his data. What matters here is that Soviet economists, like the economists elsewhere, have concluded that education can be an investment yielding a high rate of return.

47. Stanislav Strumilin, "The Economics of Education in the U.S.S.R.," *International Social Science Journal* (UNESCO), Vol. 14 (1962), p. 642.
48. *Ibid.*, p. 643.

11
The Demand for Education

Most people in most countries, developed as well as developing, consider education a "superior good," that is, one they want more of as their incomes increase. But not only is the "income elasticity of demand" for education positive, it is usually (though certainly not always) greater than unity. That is, as national income increases, the demand for education increases in most countries by a larger percentage.

This formulation is perhaps not quite felicitous in that it makes educational services appear as objects of consumption, although, as has been sufficiently emphasized, they can produce future benefits and may therefore be regarded as investment. Yet, though investment demand is usually shown as a function of expected rates of return and effective interest rates, there is nothing wrong with viewing it also as being influenced by national income. There is little doubt that both the consumption demand and the investment demand for education increase with national income.

Indices of the Use of Educational Services

The demand for education, in the parlance of economics, ought to be expressed in physical units. This, unfortunately, is complicated because there are so many different types, levels, and qualities of educational services. One will have to use some technique of "homogenizing" the heterogeneous services either in terms of resources (labor input, resources cost at constant prices) required to provide the services demanded or in terms of persons for whom the services are to be provided. Moreover, one will want to distinguish several variables that are likely to determine or influence the demand for education, such as the size and composition of the population (especially the size of the school-age population), national income per head, total national income, and the cost of educational services (in money and relative to other products).

The best-known statistical studies have exhibited, among others, the following series of data:

1. the total number of students (at various levels and grades)

THE DEMAND FOR EDUCATIONAL SERVICES

2. the number of school days per year
3. the number of students compared with the size of the population
4. the number of students compared with the size of the relevant age group (e.g., the percentage of children of school age actually attending school)
5. the ratio of students in secondary schools and higher education to those in primary schools
6. the percentages of the age group at school compared with income per head
7. the years of education embodied in the average worker in the labor force
8. the equivalent years of education (that is, years corrected for days per year) embodied in the average worker in the labor force
9. the total number of teachers
10. the number of students per teacher (the student/teacher ratio)
11. the total labor inputs for education, counting both the school personnel and the potentially employable students
12. the total labor inputs used in education compared with the total labor force
13. the total money outlays per student compared with gross national product per head

14. the total money outlays per teacher compared with gross national product per head
15. the total resources cost, explicit and implicit, of education
16. the total resources cost of education compared with consumer income, national income, or gross national product (GNP).

This is undoubtedly a very incomplete list of the data employed to indicate educational growth in growing economies. I do not expect the reader to be curious enough to want illustrations of all types of statistical analyses available, but he may want to have a taste of some of the published evidence.

International Comparisons

The relationship between income per head and percentage of school-age population actually in school can be measured by time-series analysis for a particular country or by cross-section analysis for a large group of countries. Hector Correa presented a cross-section analysis of forty-eight countries on all continents. His data showed for 1958 (or the year closest to it) annual incomes per head ranging from $45 (Burma) to $2,095 (United States of America), and percentages of children five to fourteen years old enrolled in school ranging from

1 (Nepal) to 88 (Ireland). He then took a linear regression of the enrollment ratio on income and obtained a positive regression coefficient and a significant correlation coefficient, clearly indicating that the demand for education increases when income per head increases. Observing the data for different countries scattered along a logarithmic curve, he concluded that the demand increases rapidly for low income levels but "tends to stabilize itself afterwards."[1] The same analyst found also that compulsory schooling is far less significant than income in determining actual school attendance.[2]

Another investigator, Michael Kaser, was less ambitious in that his research did not include developing countries but concentrated on twelve industrialized market economies; yet, at the same time he was much more ambitious in that his international statistics comprised a time range of between 60 and 110 years.[3] He thus combined cross-section and time-series analysis: for each of the countries, he obtained between eight and twelve observations, though not concerning all the variables that he wanted to compare with GNP per head.

1. Correa, *Economics of Human Resources*, p. 77.
2. *Ibid.*, p. 81.
3. Michael C. Kaser, "Education and Economic Progress: Experience in Industrialized Market Economies," in E. A. G. Robinson and J. E. Vaizey, eds., *The Economics of Education* (London: Macmillan; New York: St. Martin's Press, 1966), pp. 89–173.

EDUCATION AND ECONOMIC GROWTH

It hardly needs saying that practically all indices of educational services, outlays, and efforts are positively related to GNP per head. The same data, incidentally, were made, in Kaser's study, to serve double duty: without time lag, the data are interpreted as indications of the income elasticity of demand for education; used with a ten-year lag and a reversal of the causal direction, they are allowed to suggest the effect of educational efforts upon economic growth.[4]

Kaser made a peculiar choice of indices for the quantity of educational services: instead of using the more usual ratios of the number of pupils and students to the size of certain relevant age groups, he preferred to compare the number of students with the size of the entire population, and the numbers of secondary-school students and of university students with the number of primary-school students. These indices are, however, to a large extent determined by the age composition of the population and, hence, show neither the effects of rising incomes upon attendance of school at various levels nor the effects of school attendance upon the growth of income. If, for example, the percentage of students in the Swedish population was 15 between 1880 and 1910 but only 11 in 1940 and 1950, one may hardly attribute the decline to anything but a change in the birth rate and

4. *Ibid.*, pp. 109–117.

THE DEMAND FOR EDUCATIONAL SERVICES

the resulting decline in the ratio of the school-age population. Similar changes probably account for the declines from 19 to 16 which Germany experienced in the

TABLE 1
NUMBER OF STUDENTS IN SECONDARY SCHOOL
PER 1,000 PUPILS IN PRIMARY SCHOOL

Country	1900 or 1901	1920 or 1921	1937 or 1938	1940 or 1941	1946 or 1947	1950 or 1951	1958, 1959, or 1960
Belgium	45	61	100		102		264
Canada				132		172	
England and Wales*	17	58	91			433	517
France		58			156		199
Germany (present territory)		121	121				230
Japan	29	172		342	470	649	613
Netherlands	28	41	112				298
Norway	60	76			151	122	183
Sweden	26	47		93		177	
U.S.A.†	35	114		350		295	307

SOURCE: Michael C. Kaser, "Education and Economic Progress: Experience in Industrialized Market Economies," in E. A. G. Robinson and J. E. Vaizey, eds., *The Economics of Education* (London: Macmillan; New York: St. Martin's Press, 1966), pp. 89–173.

* The series for England and Wales is confined to state schools.

† Since the earlier statistical series for the United States separate public secondary- and primary-schools but give combined data for nonpublic secondary- and primary-schools, the figures in the above table are confined to public schools only (including kindergarten).

69

percentage of students in its population once from 1922 to 1932 and again from 1951 to 1959.

Table 1 presents for ten advanced countries the numbers of secondary-school students per 1,000 pupils in primary school. The increases are remarkable over the forty to sixty years for which the data are available. The record numbers for Japan deserve special attention. They evidently show that national policies and attitudes may play a very great role in the explanation of secondary-school enrollment. Note that Japan not only has been in the lead since 1947 but was actually far ahead of all other countries as far back as 1920, although its national income and GNP per head were the lowest of the entire group. The slight decline in the relative enrollment figure from 1950 to 1958 (and the much larger decline that would be seen if the year 1955 were included in the series) is evidently a result of a change in age composition. One may assume that age composition accounts also for the decline in the ratio of secondary to primary enrollment figures for the United States from 1940 to 1950. The role of growing incomes per head in explaining rising enrollment figures in secondary schools is rather obvious. But, since other factors unrelated to income are clearly of importance, I see no value in computations of regression coefficients for a mixture of different countries.

TABLE 2

NUMBER OF STUDENTS IN COLLEGES AND UNIVERSITIES PER 1,000 PUPILS IN PRIMARY SCHOOL

Country	1900 or 1901	1920 1921 or 1922	1937 or 1938	1940 or 1941	1946 or 1947	1950 or 1951	1958, 1959, or 1960
Australia*	3	6			34		32
Belgium	7	9	11		16		32
Canada	6	12		19		32	
England and Wales†		6	9			20	20
France	5	10			26		28
Germany (present territory)	6	13	10				41
Italy	10	11		29		32	35
Japan	4	8		18	31	21	48
Netherlands	4	9	11				26
Norway	4	6			29	23	15
Sweden	4	8		12		17	
U.S.A.‡	16	31		79		142	131

SOURCE: Michael C. Kaser, "Education and Economic Progress: Experience in Industrialized Market Economies," in E. A. G. Robinson and J. E. Vaizey, eds., *The Economics of Education* (London: Macmillan; New York: St. Martin's Press, 1966), pp. 89–173.

* Since the Australian statistics separate private and state schools but do not separate primary and secondary schools, the figures in the above series refer to the number of university students per 1,000 students in state primary and secondary schools.

† The series for England and Wales is confined to state primary schools (including underaged children).

‡ The series for the United States compares college and university students with pupils in public primary schools (including kindergarten). The figures, moreover, are not really comparable with those of other countries, because the first year (or first two years) of undergraduate education in many institutions of higher education in the United States are often on a level comparable to the last years of secondary education in some other countries.

The fact that the ratio of secondary-school students to primary-school pupils is much higher in England and Wales (517) than in the United States (307) has often been commented upon. Yet, if we examine Table 2, the ratios of students in higher education to primary-school pupils in twelve different countries, and note that this ratio is very much higher in the United States (131) than in England and Wales (20), we may wonder how much of the variations can be accounted for by differences in the institutional delineations between high school and "higher" education. If we made a statistical transfer, switching all American students in the first year or the first two years of college into the category of secondary-school students, the differences in the ratio might vanish or at least become inconspicuous.

Comparing the Quality of Education

As their incomes increase, people demand not only more education but also better education. Unfortunately, little progress has been made in measuring or estimating the quality of education. If one assumes that the quality of teaching is reflected in how much the students learn, one will place great emphasis on achievement tests; but then one may discount the results on the ground that a student's achievement depends perhaps more on his

THE DEMAND FOR EDUCATIONAL SERVICES

teachability than on the performance of his teachers; and often the student's teachability depends on his parents' attitudes as well as on social, ethnic, religious, and national characteristics. These things have thus far resisted measurement.

Consequently, most evaluations of the quality of teaching have disregarded comparisons of output and have concentrated on various inputs, especially numbers and quality of teachers. Among the proposed indices have been the education of the teachers (chiefly measured by the length of the teachers' formal education), the relative salaries paid to the teachers (relative to the incomes earned by high-quality talent in their respective countries), and the student/teacher ratio. Statistics of the years of education embodied in the average teacher are, to my knowledge, not available on a country basis. Salary statistics have been examined, but the problems involved are very complex. (To see this, one has only to realize that the ratio of teachers' compensation to national income per head is often highest in the least developed countries, but that this fact says little of the quality of these relatively well paid teachers.) The student/teacher ratio is the most widely used index of quality of education.

The underlying assumption, of course, is that the effectiveness of a teacher is inversely proportional to the size of the group taught. Dozens of qualifications can be raised regarding this assumption. Yet, with traditional methods of teaching, the assumption is, by and large, justified.

Table 3 presents, to the extent that comparative data are available, the student/teacher ratios for eleven advanced countries. The numbers of students and of teachers are shown in the rows above the ratios of students to teachers. These data are given (*a*) for primary schools, (*b*) for primary and secondary schools together (which, because of the wide differences in the character of secondary schools, affords more comparability than the data for secondary schools alone), and (*c*) for higher education. The series comprises four years within a period of approximately sixty years: (1) 1900 or 1901, (2) 1920, 1921, or 1922, (3) 1937, 1938, 1940, or 1941, and (4) 1958, 1959, 1960, or 1961. As no regression analysis is intended, but only rough comparisons of general trends, it does not matter much that the data are not for the same years.

For primary schools the number of students per teacher was conspicuously reduced in all countries for which information is available, except in the Netherlands. (There the ratio for 1938 was higher than that for 1900, and the ratio for 1960 was above that for 1920.) The record achievement is that of Sweden, both in terms of

TABLE 3
NUMBER OF STUDENTS PER TEACHER
(Numbers of Students and Teachers in Thousands)

		Primary Schools				Primary plus Secondary Schools				Higher Education			
		1900 or 1901	1920 1921 or 1922	1937 1938 1940 or 1941	1958 1959 1960 or 1961	1900 or 1901	1920 1921 or 1922	1937 1938 1940 or 1941	1958 1959 1960 or 1961	1900 or 1901	1920 1921 or 1922	1937 1938 1940 or 1941	1958 1959 1960 or 1961
Australia	Students	n.a.	n.a.	n.a.	n.a.	787	1,018	1,186x	1,663y	1.6	4.9	30.5	29.4
	Teachers	n.a.	n.a.	n.a.	n.a.	22.5	34.9	45.3x	36.8y	0.1	0.5	2.0	3.3
	Ratio					35.0	29.2	26.2	29.3	16.0	9.8	15.3	8.9
Belgium	Students	794	968	960	890	829.6	1,026.8	1,056.3	1,125.0	5.3	8.7	10.3	28.3
	Teachers	16.6	26.9	34.5	n.a.	n.a.	n.a.	n.a.	n.a.	n.a.	n.a.	n.a.	n.a.
	Ratio	47.8	36.0	27.8									
Canada p	Students	n.a.	n.a.	n.a.	n.a.	1,092.7	1,894.7	2,131	4,708	6.9	23.1	36	114
	Teachers	n.a.	n.a.	n.a.	n.a.	27.8	55.9	75.7	159.3	0.4	3.1	3.7	9.6
	Ratio					39.3	33.9	28.2	29.6	17.3	7.5	9.7	11.9
England and Wales p	Students	5,768	5,893	5,123	4,508	5,866	6,234	5,589	6,839	n.a.	35	45	90
	Teachers	119	165	168	148	132	187	250	258	n.a.	2		9
	Ratio	48.5	35.7	30.5	30.5	44.4	33.3	22.4	26.5		17.5	15.0	10.0
Germany (present territory)	Students	8,966	8,930	7,791	4,790	n.a.	10,011	8,734	5,891	51	120	76	196
	Teachers	147	198	183	129	n.a.	252	236	183	3	6	7	8
	Ratio	61.0	45.1	42.6	37.1		39.7	37.0	32.2	17.0	20.0	10.8	24.5
Italy v	Students	2,733	4,267	5,100	4,676	2,825	4,656	6,072	6,489	27	49	146	164
	Teachers	66	109	121	192	73	135	202	340	n.a.	2	4	6
	Ratio	41.4	39.1	42.1	24.4	38.7	34.5	30.1	19.1		24.5	36.5	27.3
Japan	Students	4,707	8,699	12,539	13,492	4,844	10,195	16,833	21,759	19	73	226	649
	Teachers	93.5	187.9	314.5	364.0	99.2	204.5	352.4	704.3	2.6	5.8	17.1	69.4
	Ratio	50.3	46.3	39.9	37.1	48.8	49.9	47.8	31.0	7.3	12.6	13.2	9.4
Netherlands	Students	740	1,032	1,143	1,481	761	1,074	1,271	1,922	3	9	13	38
	Teachers	20.6	35.3	30.1	43.3	n.a.	n.a.	38.5	64.3	0.2	0.6	0.9	1.6
	Ratio	35.9	29.2	38.0	34.2			33.0	29.9	15.0	15.0	14.4	23.7
Norway	Students	336.2	385.8	n.a.	437.3	356.3	415.2	n.a.	517.3	1.4	2.3	n.a.	6.6
	Teachers	7.3	11.1	n.a.	15.5	8.8	12.9	n.a.	19.5	0.1	0.2	n.a.	1.2
	Ratio	46.1	34.8		28.2	40.5	32.2		26.5	14.0	11.5		5.5
Sweden	Students	752.9	743.0	656.0	665.7z	772.3	777.6	716.8	783.7z	2.7	5.8	7.6	11.1z
	Teachers	16.0	26.4	30.4	36.9z	17.4	28.5	34.4	44.7z	0.3	0.4	0.8	1.5z
	Ratio	47.1	28.1	21.6	18.0	44.4	27.3	20.8	17.5	9.0	14.5	9.5	7.4
U.S.A. p	Students	14,984	19,378	18,832	27,602	15,503	21,578	25,433	36,087	238	598	1,494	3,610
	Teachers	n.a.	n.a.	n.a.	n.a.	423	680	875	1,387	24	49	147	345
	Ratio					36.7	31.7	29.1	26.0	9.9	12.2	10.2	10.5

SOURCE: Michael C. Kaser, "Education and Economic Progress: Experience in Industrialized Market Economies," in E. A. G. Robinson and J. E. Vaizey, eds., *The Economics of Education* (London: Macmillan; New York: St. Martin's Press, 1966), pp. 89–173.
p public schools only; v vocational schools included among secondary; x 1947; y 1954; z 1950.

the trend over the entire period and in terms of the low ratio attained in 1958. (This increase in the demand for improved education, incidentally, fits in well with the exceptionally fast increase and high level in Sweden's national income per head.) Only one other country, Italy, has attained a student/teacher ratio of less than 25. (Here, however, one cannot reasonably claim this ratio as the result of high income per head.) The progress in Italy took place in the last seventeen years of the period, whereas England and Wales had their progressive times in the first thirty-six years, making no further improvement on this score between 1937 and 1958. The highest student/teacher ratio of this group of countries at the beginning of the century was that of Germany, with 61.0 students per teacher; even in 1960, Germany still had the highest ratio (37.1), though tied by Japan for this poor record.

The number of students per teacher is ordinarily much lower on the secondary level. The data of Table 3 bear this out, as they show lower ratios for primary and secondary combined than for primary alone, with a single exception: Japan in 1920 and 1940. This anomaly was particularly conspicuous in 1940. Evidently, enrollment in secondary schools in Japan had been so sharply stepped up that the recruitment of teachers could not keep up with the influx of students. Progress was made

THE DEMAND FOR EDUCATIONAL SERVICES

in later years and the perverse ratios (i.e., ratios higher than for primary schools) had disappeared by 1960, though the ratio was still high relative to that of other countries; indeed, it was the second highest after Germany. Other countries with high student/teacher ratios on the primary plus secondary levels were Canada and Australia (where the ratios had increased in the last interval shown in the table). The lowest ratio, 17.5, was, not surprisingly, in Sweden; the second lowest, 19.1, rather surprisingly, was in Italy. For the United States consistent improvement is shown from 36.7 in 1900 to 26.0 in 1960.

In higher education we can see the greatest variations in trends and present levels. Norway and Sweden lead with ratios of 5.5 and 7.4, respectively. Japan, Australia, England and Wales, the United States, and Canada follow with student/teacher ratios of about 10. Three countries, however, have very high ratios: the Netherlands, 23.7; Germany, 24.5; and Italy, 27.3. In Italy the ratio had been even higher—36.5 in 1941—but in Germany and the Netherlands the ratios had greatly deteriorated. These were evidently cases of rapid increase in the demand for university education without adequate provision for professorial appointments to keep reasonable proportions. The thesis that under conditions of economic growth the demand for improved education and, hence, for reduced student/teacher ratios would steadily increase is therefore not borne out by the data for higher education. Perhaps the demand did increase, but the supply was unresponsive because of certain rigidities in the management of the university systems. In none of the ten countries for which relevant data are available can we see the consistent decline of student/teacher ratios over the years that would conform to the hypothesis. This is quite unlike the situation that we have observed in primary or secondary education.[5]

Educational Growth in the United States

Much research has been done on educational growth in the United States, and some of the results ought to be reported here.

5. The data for entire countries conceal the very large differences in student/teacher ratios among various institutions of higher education, particularly in the United States. The most prestigious private universities regard research as one of their primary objectives. The greater emphasis on research explains much lower student/teacher ratios in these institutions. The implications for the quality of education are controversial, since only the teaching loads of the professors but not the number of students in their courses may be reduced. Some observers believe that the research interests of the professors compete with their teaching efforts. Others, however, hold that the productive researcher is also a more effective teacher, so that the low student/teacher ratio would still indicate higher quality of higher education.

THE DEMAND FOR EDUCATIONAL SERVICES

The relationship between aggregate national income, or GNP, and total expenditures for education has been most keenly observed. This is understandable even if this ratio cannot legitimately be used for measurements on the income elasticity of demand for education. The statistical findings have rather consistently confirmed the generalization that educational expenditures grow faster than GNP. This has been true for money expenditures and, with an even faster rate of growth, for total cost incurred for education, including implicit costs such as incomes foregone by older students attending school instead of taking jobs.

My own calculations have shown that from 1948 to 1958, when the gross national product of the United States increased at an annual rate of about 5.9 percent (at current prices), money outlays for elementary and secondary education increased by 12 percent per year.[6] The rate of growth of monetary plus implicit costs of higher education has probably been even greater, especially if the time series is extended into the late 1960s.

T. W. Schultz has provided a number of interesting calculations comparing educational efforts with economic growth in the United States over long periods of time. "Labor inputs in education" (teachers and employable students) were 5.3 percent of the employed labor

6. Machlup, *Production and Distribution*, p. 370.

force in 1900, but 18.8 percent in 1956. "Gross resources cost (at current prices)" of schooling was 2.9 percent of consumer income in 1900, but 10.3 percent in 1956. According to his calculation, "a 1 percent increase in real per capita income was associated with a 3.5 percent increase in the allocation of resources to education."[7] When he inquired into the steady increase in the number of school years completed by members of the labor force, he found that his first results understated the progress made in that school days per year had risen considerably over the years. In 1900 average attendance was 99 days a year; in 1940, 152 days; and in 1957, 159 days. To adjust the number of school years completed for differences in average attendance, he took the attendance figure for 1940 as a standard, named "equivalent school year." His adjusted time series of years of school completed per member of the labor force gives the number of equivalent school years completed as 4.14 in 1900, 5.25 in 1920, 7.24 in 1940, and 10.45 in 1957.[8]

Disentangling Increases in Demand and in Cost

Since many of the statistical series compare national outlays for education with national income and may suggest that the ratios obtained measure the demand for

7. Schultz, "Education and Economic Growth," p. 60.
8. *Ibid.*, pp. 67–68.

THE DEMAND FOR EDUCATIONAL SERVICES

education, or indicate the income elasticity of demand, one should warn against such suggestions. Outlays are a combined result of cost and demand, and only if the supply of educational services were infinitely elastic (that is, if the cost per student were constant) would increased outlays measure increased demand. If the supply is not perfectly elastic, an increase in outlay will depend not only on the increase in demand but also on the elasticity of supply and on the elasticity of demand; and there is no reliable way to separate these three constituents of total outlay.

The disentanglement is particularly difficult because the increase in income that raises the demand for education may at the same time reduce the price-elasticity of demand and increase the major cost items that enter into the supply curve of educational services. Thus, an *increase in national income* will lead to a more than proportional *increase in the demand for education* and at the same time, for reasons to be explained in the next section, to an upward shift (decline) in the supply curve for educational services; with a relatively inelastic demand, the higher price of educational services must result in an *increase in total outlays for education* more than proportional to the increase in demand.

Statistical measurements to test these theoretical propositions are hardly possible, but are not very important either. Any numerical results for one period will not apply to another period, numerical estimates will differ from country to country, and the results of aggregations of different countries have little meaning. The only practical conclusion from our generalizations is that governments should brace themselves for the hard realization of rapid increases in expenditures for education.

III
The Cost of Education

If the products of education were measurable, say, in bits of information received, amounts of knowledge absorbed, or potential intellectual and moral energy stored up, discussions of changes in the cost of education would make much better sense. As it is, we can measure at best the inputs that society employs to supply educational services to certain numbers of students, that is, to expose certain numbers of people to schooling or instruction of some sort for a certain number of hours per year.

If society's demand for education is measured by what society spends on education, and if these expenditures are represented as the cost of education, we have arrived at a sterile tautology, where demand and cost mean exactly the same. Yet, the proposition that the *cost* of education has been increasing and is expected to increase further surely means more than that society's *demand* for education has been increasing and will increase further.

Total Expenditures, Cost of a Given Task, Cost per Unit

In still simpler words: If people buy more of a thing or service, perhaps also of a better quality, they usually have to pay more for it. With their expenditures thus increased, they sometimes say afterwards that the "cost" of that budget item has increased. This is sloppy speech, if not self-deception; in a strict sense of the word, cost has increased only if one has to pay more for a specified quantity of an unchanged quality.

I do not mean to scold those of us who have spoken of the "cost of education" in a country when we meant the actual inputs used for the total of educational services actually provided. I merely want to show the importance of developing concepts which distinguish this notion of cost from other ideas indispensable in economic analysis, for example, cost in the sense of the productive or financial resources required for stated "specified" amounts of educational services. Unfortunately, the variety of relevant specifications is greater than can be accommodated by a simple conceptual framework; a somewhat complicated set of concepts is needed.

THE COST OF EDUCATION

Complications arise for a variety of reasons, among the most obvious of which are changes in the size of the population, changes in the age composition of the population (increasing, for example, the school-age population relative to the total, or the ratios of children of secondary-school age to those of primary-school age), changes in the rates of school attendance among given age groups, and changes in the teaching efforts and facilities required to achieve given standards of achievement in fields in which knowledge advances fast.

One may hold that some of these changes are inconsistent with the postulate of a "specified amount of education." If the number of students in secondary school increases because there are more children in the particular age group, one will surely agree that the resulting increase in cost be recognized as the "required" cost of a "given task"; however, if the number increases because a larger percentage of persons in this age group decides to attend secondary school, or to stay there a few more years, one may say that this represents an increase in the demand for education. On the other hand, one can argue that changes in technology have raised the prerequisites of employability and that it is a given task of the school system to turn out employable members of the labor force; the additional cost due to the increased enrollment rate would then qualify as a legitimate cost item.

The issues are similar regarding increased requirements in rapidly advancing subjects, for instance, physics and biology. One may argue that to disseminate the most up-to-date state of knowledge is a given task of the school system and, if better teachers, more expensive facilities, or lower student/teacher ratios are needed to do this task, one ought to characterize the resulting expenditures as constituting increased cost of providing a given amount of education.

For my taste the sophistication of some of these arguments comes close to sophistry. If little Johnny contends that he "needs" a motorcycle because his bicycle is too slow, we can reasonably leave it to him to persuade his parents that the money he wants is neither for consumption nor investment but reflects an increase in the cost of transportation. We need not take sides, and especially need not declare ourselves for or against the purchase of the more expensive vehicle. Likewise, in the discussion of whether increased enrollment rates in secondary schools and colleges constitute additional consumption, investment, or increased cost of a given amount of education, we are not arguing for or against the outlays involved. All we want is comprehension of what is being said, and we can understand these matters better if we construe the given educational task narrowly and are explicit in specifying any expansion of the task,

THE COST OF EDUCATION

however desirable or necessary for the attainment of individual or social objectives.

We conclude that increases in the total expenditures for education that are due to increased enrollment rates, reduced student/teacher ratios, improved educational facilities (libraries, laboratories), or improved noneducational facilities (stadiums for spectator sports) should not be merged with such additions to expenditures as are associated with changes in the age composition of the population, changes in the salaries required to obtain the needed number of teachers, or changes in the incomes foregone by (given percentages of) students of employable ages. The proposed separation will help distinguish additions to the educational budget that can more reasonably be attributed to increased demand from those additions that are caused by inevitable increases in the cost of providing educational services of a given scope.

Cost per unit is usually the most convenient way of examining changes of cost over time. The unit in which the average cost of education is most clearly expressed is the student (student-hour or student-year). But since it is much less expensive to teach reading to first-graders than biology to high-school juniors, and this again is much less expensive than teaching physics to university students, cost per student of an unknown composition of the student population is not meaningful. Statistical disaggregation of the educational sector, at least into the four customary subsystems—primary, secondary, vocational, and higher (university) education—is a prerequisite of a good cost analysis. (Further disaggregations would be desirable but are impossible because of joint costs and overhead expenditures.) Detailed classifications of cost items according to teaching personnel, administration, buildings and grounds, laboratories, libraries, supplies, auxiliary services, and implicit costs (especially earnings foregone by employable students) are very significant for thorough analyses.

Cost per student at a particular school level is, however, not the only unit cost used in comparative studies of education. Various statistical researchers have computed the cost of education per head (of the entire population) and the share of educational services in gross national product. (It should be understood that the latter fraction is identical with the ratio of the cost of education per head to GNP per head.) Another measure that may serve purposes of international comparison is the cost of education per person of school age.

Scrambled Measures of Cost

Most of the alternative measures of the cost of education—virtually all except the cost per student at a particular level of schooling—are primarily reflections,

THE COST OF EDUCATION

not of cost in the strict sense, but of a variety of other factors, too. They reflect some demographic and social differences (international or over time) and, mainly, differences in demand.

Assume, for purposes of illustration, that costs per student at primary school, secondary school, vocational school, and in higher education stay unchanged at their respective values for several years. A temporary increase in the birth rate would increase the relative number of pre-school children, which would reduce the cost of education per head. A few years later, as the wave of new births transforms itself into a wave of primary-school enrollment, the cost of education per head would rise above the initial value. It would continue to rise as the crest of the flood moves on to the secondary and vocational school systems and finally to colleges and universities. In the unlikely case that during this period GNP remains unchanged, the ratio of educational expenditures to GNP would have been unaffected during the first few years but increased for the subsequent twelve to sixteen years.

Again assuming that the costs per student stay unchanged at each level, let us suppose that it becomes "the thing to do" to stay two more years at secondary school and to go on to college. Cost per head of population will increase and educational expenditures as a ratio to GNP will increase likewise. The increased enrollment ratios may be due to changes in tastes but also to increasing affluence; in the latter case, the increase in the ratio of educational expenditures to GNP will, of course, be more modest.

There is the possibility in some countries that economies of size arise as enrollment increases. For example, university education can become less expensive per student if the capacity of the institutions has hitherto been underutilized. (It has been said that excess capacity is one of the reasons why the cost of university education per student is three to five times as high in several of the new African nations as in Europe.[1]) In such instances the student/teacher ratio may increase without serious impairment of quality. The reduction in the cost of higher education per student will, however, still not avoid the serious increases in the cost of education per head (and as a ratio to GNP) that are generally associated with the expansion of university enrollments.

We may come back once more to the question of the reductions in student/teacher ratios, especially in higher education. To the extent that they are associated with the broadening of university curricula, increased specialization (with professors concentrating on narrow subjects elected by only a few students), and increased

1. Lewis, *I.S.S.J.*, p. 688; *Readings*, p. 142.

emphasis on research (with the consequent need of increasing the teaching staff as each member offers fewer hours of instruction), the reduction in the student/teacher ratio ordinarily constitutes an improvement in the quality of higher education and an increase in the cost per student. Our previous argument has supported the view that these quality improvements were a matter of demand—society paying a higher price for a better product—and that the cost increase was therefore not an autonomous change in supply conditions. There are two considerations, however, which may cast a somewhat different light on the development.

One of these considerations shifts the focus from the system of higher education to the individual institution. As more and more universities attempt to meet the demand for higher quality, by broadening their curricula and by providing more opportunity for research, individual institutions may soon find that they have no choice: in order to go on, they have to meet the higher standards. For the individual institution the cost of education per student will have increased, and the administration can do nothing but accept the higher cost of instruction. This is not inconsistent with the assumption that the chain of events may have started from higher incomes and an elastic demand for the better things. (It is analogous to the causal chain in which we go from higher incomes by way of higher standards of living to higher costs of living.)

A similar consideration concerns the supply of qualified academic teachers. The increased emphasis upon scholarly research has made research and publications the most recognized criteria of academic qualification, promotion, and career prospects. This in turn has made academic teachers unwilling to accept positions that do not afford them ample time for research and writing. The supply of university teachers prepared to teach nine or twelve hours a week has been drying up, and the colleges and universities are more and more confined to a supply of teachers offering no more than six teaching hours a week. This represents a reduction in student/teacher ratios and an increase in the cost per student that leave the institutions no way out. For higher education this is a real autonomous increase in cost.

Human Costs Rising with Economic Growth

The most perpetual, inexorably persistent force in the secular rise in the cost of education on all levels is the continuing increase in the earnings of teachers (and potential earnings of older students) as they keep up with the average rise of earnings in a growing economy. If salaries failed to keep approximate pace with the

THE COST OF EDUCATION

incomes earned in other occupations, the number of teachers in the educational labor force would soon begin to fall.

The increase of earnings of labor, measured in terms of real goods, is of course one of the fundamental characteristics of economic growth. It is a corollary of the continual increase in the quantities of material products that can be produced per unit of labor. Productivity per unit of labor rises at very different rates in different industries; it advances one year in one sector, another year in another, sometimes in agriculture, at other times in mining, most often in manufacturing; and, in a market economy, the average increase in productivity determines the average increase in real wages and salaries in the economy. Wages and salaries must rise also in those sectors where productivity fails to increase—otherwise workers would leave these sectors and try to get the jobs of the workers in the industries where productivity advances.

The argument has nothing to do either with trade-union power or with monetary inflation; but, since it has become rather difficult to imagine a situation in which neither of the two makes its presence felt, let us assume, to simplify the reasoning, that the trade unions have consented not to push up money wages at a rate faster than the average rate of increase of productivity in the production of real goods, and that the fiscal and monetary authorities have the wisdom to keep monetary expansion within the limits required to avoid pulling up prices and wages. In such circumstances, the price level of real goods will remain stable: production per worker is larger, but money-wage rates increase in the same proportion. If wage rates, contrary to our assumption, remained unchanged, labor cost per unit of output would be reduced by, say, 3 percent a year, thanks to the larger output per worker. With money-wage rates increased by 3 percent a year, the same rate at which output per worker increases, labor cost per unit of output would remain unchanged.

So much about the sectors producing physical goods. What happens in the sectors in which techniques of production do not change? What happens, in particular, in the production of educational services? The answer holds serious implications, for, since wages and salaries must increase there as everywhere else while these increases are not offset by any increase in productivity per worker, the cost of the services, that is, the cost per student at any level of education, must increase year after year. On our assumption of a 3-percent rate of increase of physical productivity and of money rates of earning, the cost per student must increase by approximately 3 percent every year.[2]

2. I am disregarding here the fact that some physical goods (equipment, fuel, etc.) are used in the production of educational

THE COST OF EDUCATION

Comparing the two sectors of the economy, we note that physical goods will be sold, thanks to the increase in productivity per worker, in ever-increasing quantities at stable prices, whereas educational services, produced with an unchanged output per teacher, will cost more and more and more.[3]

Let us repeat that this continual increase in the cost of education per student is not a consequence of inflation; if there is inflation, the rate of increase will be that much greater. The continual increase in costs is the inevitable result of two facts: (1) economic growth, that is, increasing productivity per worker in the production of physical goods and services, and (2) absence of technological improvement in the provision of education. If the technology of education remains unchanged—so that no more students than now can be taught per teacher—the cost of education per student must increase in perpetuity, and the rate of increase will vary directly with the rate of economic growth.

The portent of this situation has recently been elucidated by William Baumol.[4] Let "education" stand for

---

services. In other words, I am concentrating on the personnel cost of instruction.

3. I first discussed these differences between physical goods and intangible services in my *Production and Distribution*, pp. 374–76.

4. William J. Baumol, "Macroeconomics of Unbalanced Growth: The Anatomy of Urban Crisis," *American Economic Review*, Vol. 57 (June 1967), pp. 415–25.

all products in which productivity remains unchanged, and "physical product" for all the goods that are produced with gradually increasing productivity per worker. Then we can deduce the following propositions:

1. The cost of education per student will rise without limit, relative to the cost per unit of physical product.
2. If the demand for education is elastic with respect to price (so that less will be "bought" at higher prices) and inelastic with respect to income (so that no more will be "bought" at higher incomes), the supply of education will vanish.
3. If the conditions of demand are not as was hypothecated in the previous proposition, but instead are such that the ratios of output of education to physical product are to be kept constant, this will require perpetual transfers of labor from physical production to education.
4. Since such transfers continually reduce the ratio of workers in the sector in which productivity increases, the rate of economic growth must steadily decline and approach zero.

As in most cases of exponential growth, the developments will never reach the hypothetical limit, because a practical-political limit is likely to intervene much earlier. Society would not let the supply of education vanish,

THE COST OF EDUCATION

nor would it allocate an ever-growing share of its manpower to education, thereby denuding its sector of physical production. But if society resists the perpetual increase in the cost of education per student and yet cannot resist paying to teachers the same annual increases in earnings that arise in physical production, where is a way out of the dilemma? There is one possible escape: changing the technology of teaching, probably through automation.

Growth with Inflation

Our assumption that there are no inflationary push-ups and pull-ups of incomes and prices has served only a didactic purpose. The assumption really makes no difference to the basic conclusion that the *real earnings* of those engaged in education—the earnings received by teachers and the earnings foregone by employable students—must rise as long as economic growth continues. The fact that most nations are pursuing monetary and fiscal policies conducive to continual inflation of incomes and prices has its chief implication for the *money cost* of education. If real income per head increases by, say, 3 percent a year, but money income per head increases by, say, 6 percent, the national accounts in current dollars will of course reflect the higher rate of increase.

The educational institutions, the school systems, the political authorities in charge of budget appropriations, and the fiscal authorities must reckon with the increase in money cost. Important as it is for economic analysts to distinguish the rate of real growth and the rate of monetary inflation, those who are concerned with raising the required funds have to figure the increase that results from the combination of the two, real growth plus inflation.

The Prospects

The prospects are frightening, especially if one realizes that growth and inflation are not the only factors that will swell the education bill. Let us remember the steady increase in the percentage of young people who are put under pressure to spend a full twelve years in primary and secondary schools and the stupendous increase in the percentage of persons who are sponsored to undertake education beyond high school.

According to official estimates, the number of those enrolled in degree courses at colleges and universities in the United States will increase by more than 50 percent in ten years. If student/teacher ratios remain unchanged, the cost per student, increasing by 6 percent annually on the ground of growth plus inflation, would rise by

THE COST OF EDUCATION

80 percent in ten years. These factors alone—disregarding the cost of additional space, facilities, libraries, etc.—would raise the annual cost of higher education by 170 percent in the next decade. Estimates for a more distant future are, of course, still more awesome.[5]

Some of the published estimates extend the horizon to some forty years ahead. The projections look well-nigh astronomical. To be sure, the present expenditures for education would have looked astronomical, fantastic, and perhaps absurd to a fiscal authority about forty years ago; yet, we have come to live with these expenditures and, indeed, are doing our best to persuade political conservatives to relax their opposition to faster growth of appropriations to education. Perhaps the gigantic figures for the years 2000 or 2010 will actually materialize; but perhaps they will not, for there will be increasingly heavy competition from other civic needs and desiderata: health services, water resources, safeguards against the pollution of air and water, and many other problems of the city may make such heavy demands on the fiscal capacities of society that the pressures for economies

5. William G. Bowen, *The Economics of the Major Private Universities* (Berkeley, Calif.: Carnegie Commission on Higher Education, 1968); William J. Baumol and Peggy Heim, "On the Financial Prospects for Higher Education: The Annual Report on the Economic Status of the Profession, 1967–68," *AAUP Bulletin*, Vol. 54 (June 1968), pp. 182–96.

through technological improvements in education will be irresistible.

Most teachers today, at all levels of education, are convinced that there can be no good teaching and no effective learning without teacher personally communicating with student, indeed, without meaningful dialogue between student and teacher. Perhaps these are the best techniques of teaching (though I have no evidence that less personal and more mechanical or automated techniques may not in fact be superior). But this is not the question. The real question is whether society will stick to this method of teaching when alternative methods are developed that are reasonably effective and much less expensive.

I certainly shall not be around in the year 2000 or 2010 to examine the statistics of the number of students per teacher and the number of teaching machines per student and per teacher; but if I were to be around, I should not be surprised to find that capital has been substituted for labor in the area of education as it has in most other sectors of a growing economy. The faster the economy grows, the faster rises the cost of education by traditional methods and the faster will these methods be replaced by others that economize human resources.

Index

Ability and ambition, 40–41, 43–44, 47, 73
Adult Education, 27–30
Agriculture, 21, 23, 30
Africa, 90
Allocation of resources, 8, 54, 97
Annual versus hourly earnings, 48
Anderson, C. Arnold, 46 n
Australia, 71, 75, 77
Automation in teaching, 97, 100

Baumol, William J., 95, 99 n
Becker, Gary S., 41, 43–44, 55
Belgium, 69, 71, 75
Birth control, 21
Birth rates, 17–21, 68, 89
Blaug, Mark, 26 n, 47 n, 51 n

Bogota, 26 n, 45–46
Bowen, William G., 16 n, 99 n
Bowman, Mary Jean, 23 n, 36 n, 46 n, 57 n
Burma, 66

Canada, 69, 71, 75, 77
Capital, human, 13, 35, 58; physical, 7, 8, 12–14, 19, 47, 59, 60, 100
Chile, 25, 46
Colombia, 26, 45–46
Competition, 37, 52, 60, 99
Complementarity, 37
Cornoy, Martin, 46 n
Correa, Hector, 12 n, 66–67
Cost of education, 2, 64–66, 79–80, 82, 83–100; confused with demand, 80–82, 83–87, 89, 91; meaning of,

INDEX

Cost of education—*cont.*
  84–86; per student, 65, 87–88, 90
Czechoslovakia, 27

Death rates, 17–18
Demand, confused with cost, 80–82, 83–87, 89, 91; for education, 2, 63–82, 85, 87, 96; for higher education, 77–78, 98; for skilled labor, 26, 44
Denison, Edward F., 12, 41
Development versus growth, 1
Discount rate, 34
Disembodied progress, 11
Double counting of effect of education, 52–54
Dressel, Paul L., 50 n
Drop-outs, 25, 35

Elasticities of supply and demand, 81, 91, 96
Elasticity of substitution, 48–49
Emigration, 26, 45–46
Employment opportunities, 5, 23, 26; rate, 6, 13, 15, 17
England, 69, 71, 72, 75, 76 77

Envy, 34–35 n
Equivalent school year, 65, 80
Europe, 90
Exploitation, 57, 59

Finegan, T. Aldrich, 16 n, 49 n
Foreign languages, 45
France, 69, 71
Future versus immediate benefits, 5, 63

Germany, 69, 71, 75, 76, 77
Gordon, John E., 20 n
Gounden, A. M. Nalla, 46 n
Growth, factors in economic, 6–9; of education, 2, 66, 79, 81; of knowledge, 52–55; of national income, 2, 6, 10, 12–15, 52, 60–61, 63, 66–68, 70, 79, 81; of population, 17–21, 64, 85, 89; of productivity, 2, 5, 21, 42, 52, 55, 56–61; versus development, 1
Growth jobs, 29, 41–42

Haiti, 25
Hanoch, Giora, 43 n
Harberger, Arnold, 46 n, 47 n
Harbison, Frederick, 25, 27 n

INDEX

Health, 7, 18, 19, 50, 99
Heim, Peggy, 99 n
Henry, Nelson B., 12 n
Higher education and political stability, 55–56; and working hours, 47–49; cost of, 79, 87–88, 90–92; demand for, 77–78, 98; economies of size in, 90; in poor countries, 26–27; number of students in, 71–72, 89; returns from, 35, 43, 45–47, 55, 61; student/teacher ratios in, 74–75, 77–78, 91–92

Income, a function of age, 40; and demand, 2, 63–64, 66–68; distribution, 15, 38; foregone by students, 28, 29, 87, 88, 92, 97; foregone in growth jobs, 41–42
Income elasticity of demand, 63, 68, 79, 81, 96
India, 26 n, 27, 46–47
Indices of educational growth, 2, 64–68
Inflation, 93, 95, 97–98
Input and output in education, 83, 95
Input-output analysis, 51

Intelligence quotients, 40–41
Investment, in education, 5, 11–15, 30, 35–36, 53–56, 58–61, 86; in on-the-job learning, 29; in physical capital, 7, 8, 14, 47; in research, 54
Ireland, 67
Italy, 71, 75, 76, 77

Japan, 69, 70, 71, 75, 76, 77

Kaser, Michael C., 67–69, 71 n, 75 n
Komarov, V. E., 57 n
Kuznets, Simon, 9–10 n

Labor force, increase in, 6, 12, 60; influenced by education, 6–7, 15–17; participation, 7, 15–17
Labor mobility, 7, 8
Layard, Richard, 26 n, 47 n
Learning on the job, 41–42
Leisure, 6, 21, 47–49
Lewis, W. Arthur, 23–25, 29 n, 90 n

Machlup, Fritz, 5 n, 28 n, 79, 95 n

INDEX

Malnutrition, 19, 20
Management, 8, 53, 54
Manpower needs, 50–51
Marginal product, 60
Markov chains, 51 n
Marx, Karl, 59
Mathematical models, 50 n, 51 n
Measuring the effects of education, 9–15
Mexico, 25, 46
Mincer, Jacob, 42 n
Minimum wages, 44
Myers, Charles A., 25, 27 n

Nepal, 67
Netherlands, 69, 71, 74, 75, 77
Nigeria, 24
Nonpecuniary benefits, 5, 22, 34 n, 35, 50
Norway, 69, 71, 75, 77

Pay-off period, 27–30
Political stability, 24, 55–56
Pontryagin's maximum principle, 51 n
Population, age composition of, 6, 20, 39, 64, 70, 85, 87, 89; growth of, 17–21, 64, 85, 89; school-age, 64–65, 68–69, 85, 98

Preferences and tastes, 48–49, 90
Primary education, costs per student, 89; in poor countries, 24–25; rates of return to, 45–47; ratios of students in secondary education, 65, 68, 69–70; ratios of students in universities, 71–72; student/teacher ratios, 74–76
Private returns versus social, 30–34, 38–39, 44–47, 49–56
Productivity, contrasted with other values, 27, 50; due to education, 2, 5, 6–9, 21, 29, 42, 53–55, 56–61; due to improved knowledge, 52–54; increasing with age, 42; in producing physical goods, 93–97; in supplying education, 95–97; meaning of, 22; of less qualified labor, 37
Psychic income, 34 n, 48–49

Quality, of education, 72–78, 84, 90–91; of labor, 7, 8, 10, 11–14, 40–41, 58–61; of teaching and teachers, 73, 86

INDEX

Rates of return, calculations of, 43–47, 55, 56–61; for women, 45; over life time, 28, 35, 43; private versus social, 30–34, 38–39, 44–47, 49–56
Research, 78 n, 91–92; and development, 8, 11, 53–54
Residual, 11–15, 41, 50, 60
Robinson, E. Austin G., 12 n, 67 n, 69 n, 71 n, 75 n

Saving habits, 7
Schultz, Theodore P., 26 n, 45 n
Schultz, Theodore W., 11–15, 79–80
Scrimshaw, Nevin S., 20 n
Secondary education, costs per student, 89; equivalent to American college, 72; in developing countries, 24–25; rates of return to, 43–46, 61; ratios of students to those in primary school, 65, 68–70; student/teacher ratios, 74–77
Selowsky, Marcelo, 46 n
Shoup, Carl, 46 n
Smith, Joseph, 41 n

Social benefits, 31–34, 38–39, 45, 49–56
Soviet Russia, 56–61
Statistics of national income, 9; subjective judgments in, 9 n
Strumilin, Stanislav G., 56–61
Student rebellion, 55–56
Student/teacher ratio, 65, 73–78, 86–87, 90–92, 98
Sweden, 68, 69, 71, 74, 75, 76, 77

Taxes, 31, 33, 49
Teachers, salaries of, 87, 92–94, 97; supply of, 92, 93, 96
Technical progress, 8, 11, 12, 53–54, 60, 93–96
Technology of education, 95–97, 100
Thünen, Johann Heinrich von, 56
Tinbergen, Jan, 51 n
Trade unions, 93
Training on the job, 27–30

Unemployment, 23–24
United States, 43–44, 55, 66, 69, 70, 71, 72, 75, 77, 78–80, 98

INDEX

Unproductive education, 5, 21–27, 38
Uruguay, 27

Vaizey, John E., 12 n, 67 n, 69 n, 71 n, 75 n
Venezuela, 25, 46
Vocational training, 25, 30, 45, 75, 89

Wales, 69, 71, 72, 75, 76, 77
Welfare economies, 48–49
Wolfle, Dael, 41 n
Woodhall, Maureen, 26 n, 47 n
Working habits, 7, 48
Working hours, 6, 47–49

Zaidan, George C., 19 n, 20 n